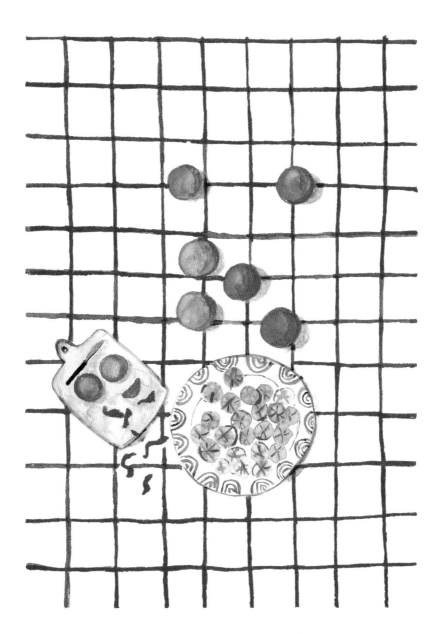

THE KITCHEN GARDEN

To my two beautiful children, Lily and Fred,
who are and always will be my inspiration.

The Kitchen Garden

Lucy Mora

Sowing, growing and cooking for the garden enthusiast

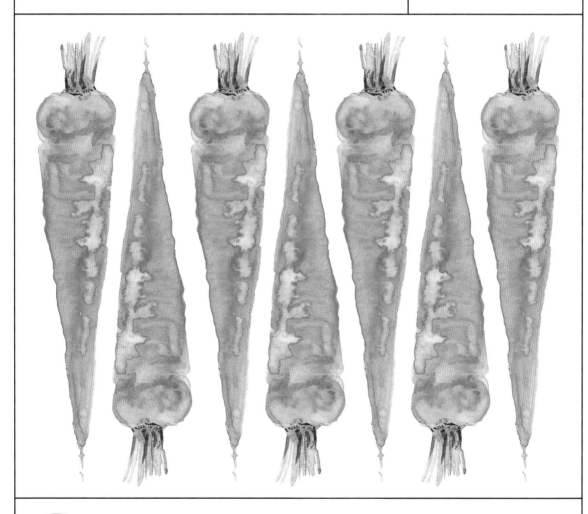

Contents

Introduction

I had an obsession with trawling for country houses after my first marriage ended. It was 'fantasy trolley' stuff as I didn't really think I'd make the move. Then one day I announced to my new partner, Julian, that we were going to inspect a house in Newstead, just an hour and a half north of Melbourne, Victoria. With no real explanation of why we were going, he kept saying, 'So, why are we going to look at this place? Are we going to buy it?'

'No, we aren't buying it. We are just going for a look.' He seemed rather confused but happy enough to be going on a country drive. I loved the house the moment I saw it. It's that feeling of huge excitement and terror at the same time. A lovely white weatherboard house with an orchard, a very grand chicken coop and a vegetable garden hemmed with a picket fence. It was when I stepped into the pantry that I knew I had to have it. We found a way to buy it and moved in.

Both of us had grown up in the country, so the change was just like going back. I grew up on a sheep and cattle property in the Southern Tablelands of New South Wales. I have wondered where my love for growing vegetables and preserving came from, as it wasn't directly from my parents. My father created a really beautiful garden, park-like with undulating lawns and established trees. He also had a love of roses, but never vegetables. My mother buckles at the idea of a vegetable garden. She loathes the idea of the abundance of it all and what to do with baskets full of tomatoes or zucchinis that grow into the size of a newborn baby. Even though she is a good and interested gardener she prefers to stick with herbs in pots when it comes to a kitchen garden.

My influences were close by in my visits to family and friends in nearby houses. Probably the most significant was my grandparents' house: they lived in a large homestead with an extensive garden. We would often meet our cousins there and my grandmother was rather formidable and insisted that children should play outside. I remember a beautiful walled garden with a long central fishpond and rows of roses; a wonderful magnolia tree with heavy white flowers hung just over the high stone wall offering a cool and dark shade.

But it was the arched doorway and an old falling-down gate that had our interest. It led us into a very different landscape: a dry path winding down the hill through the orchard, trees dripping in pears and apples, and past a wonderfully large fig tree. I was always a bit nervous about venturing out past the gate as my siblings and I were much more obedient than our wild and cheeky cousins. They were haphazard in pulling fruit from the trees, taking several bites and tossing the rest. They adored the figs, which I only pretended to like.

At the bottom of the orchard was a scene right out of a Beatrix Potter book: a large vegetable garden and potting shed with our very own version of Mr McGregor. His name was Ernie and he wore overalls and a trilby hat. I don't think I would have ever gone in there if it weren't for my cousins, who boldly raced in to see him, although it was always a complete unknown how he was going to react. Sometimes he would be happy to show off his rows of peas and carrots and break open pods of broad beans for us. But other days he would be grumpy and shoo us off like flies. I was always intrigued by his potting shed, but he never let us in there. I think this was my only experience of a vegetable garden growing up.

My obsession with preserving comes from my best friend's house. She was one of a large and happy family of six children. I stayed with her often and mealtimes were chaotic. My politeness had me not quite knowing how to behave at the dinner table. We had been taught to sit nicely; they were noisy and loud. At the end of the kitchen was an enormous dresser full of preserved fruit. Cherries, apricots, pears, nectarines, all lined up in a colourful array of Fowlers Vacola jars. At the end of the meal, I was asked (as the guest) to choose which bottle would be opened for pudding. I think I spent the entire mealtime trying to decide. No matter my choice, the fruit was always served with ice cream.

Another preserving highlight for me as a child was our annual visit to the Sydney Royal Agricultural Show. I still have vivid memories of the fruit and vegetable pavilion where the exhibitors created intricate pictures of landscapes with their produce. Celery became hedgerows, apples graded into colours became pastures and oranges made vivid sunsets. Carefully placed cherries became apples on trees and walnuts in rows made perfect garden paths. Each 'artwork' was edged with jar upon jar of preserved fruit, in beautiful mosaics of pretty patterns. These farmers must have worked hard all year with this highly competitive show in mind.

My time working as an illustrator of old and established gardens (@thegardenmapper) gave me many enjoyable hours with some of the most amazing head gardeners in Australia. It is through these conversations that my knowledge and interest in gardens grew. I am by no means a horticultural expert, just your average enthusiast. Gardeners can talk plants and how to grow them ad infinitum and I am an eager recipient of their wisdom. Knowledge is often shared under a beautiful old oak tree with a tin mug of tea and crumbly biscuit while on a morning break. I have many cuttings that were given to me during these jobs, that are nice little reminders of where they have come from.

I don't think anyone actually feels they are ahead of their game in their garden. It tugs on you to do more. There are, however, wonderful moments that make you truly happy when you catch a glimpse of what you've set out to achieve and there it is in all its glory: it fills you with joy.

I wrote this book to share that enthusiasm and, I hope, to spark others to have a go and not feel daunted by doing so. In this book, I share my collected experiences and favourite varieties, but there is always more to learn and new varieties to grow. I still marvel at anything I grow; each eggplant or tomato is held up with pride. To eat a plate of food that has entirely come from your own backyard is almost certainly one of the greatest pleasures in life.

Chapter 01

Springtime planting

A lot happens in the springtime garden, and as the weather improves gardeners are itching to get into it. We get our first hints of spring in the nearby bush with explosions of beautiful yellow wattle: I feel it lifts everyone's spirits. It's closely followed by daffodils and blossom trees, with our almond tree being a front runner. My favourites are the heavy-blossomed quince tree, and the euphorbia that jumps up with its iridescent lime green heads. I know when we see the asparagus spears forge through that finally spring is here. It's at this stage that it's full steam ahead with garden planning and soil preparation. The list of vegetables that can be planted is suddenly very long; however, there is still the chance of severe frosts so care needs to be taken in protecting those that aren't frost hardy. Start seedlings off on warm windowsills or in the greenhouse until the second month of spring. Timing is tricky at this point as baby seedlings are lined up ready to plant and winter crops are still doing their thing. Sometimes a crop needs to be sacrificed to make way for another. Spring is definitely the busiest time in the garden and possibly the most enjoyable. It's a matter of getting your summer crops in (don't miss this window) and getting on top of all the weeds.

Artichokes

⚘	**Sow** spring
◎	**Harvest** spring, summer
◷	**Growing time** 6–8 weeks (after transplanting) or 64 weeks (from seed)
♥♥	**Space between plants** 1.5 m
▽	**Pots** no
☼	**Aspect** full sun
⏚	**Soil pH** 6.8–7.5
❋	**Frost tolerant** yes
♡	**Companions** broccoli, Brussels sprouts, cabbage, cauliflower, kohlrabi, turnips
◠	**Dislikes** none

Varieties

Globe – reliable, good yield
Romanesco – small yield, good flavour
Violet de Provence – strong flavour

Sow

Sow seeds into prepared seed trays (see p. 165) to the depth of 2 cm and 2 cm apart. When the seedlings are in leaf you can prick them out and pot into 15 cm pots.

Plant out into well-prepared soil (see p. 158) when roots reach the bottom of the pot. Plants need to be 1–1.5 metres apart.

Nurture

Keep plants well watered when they are young. The plants will become quite drought tolerant once established. After harvest the plant can be cut down to the ground and it will re-emerge in the next season.

Harvest

Harvest when the globes are a good size, approximately the size of a large orange. Use a sharp knife to slice off just below the central globe. The side globes will then develop for a later harvest.

Artichokes grown from seed will only yield in their second year. They are perennial plants so they will keep coming back year after year, up to four years. They need to be cut to the ground at the end of autumn and new shoots in spring should be fertilised with a slow-release fertiliser.

Stuffed artichokes

This recipe comes from a dear friend of mine, author Diana Georgeff, who is a superb cook. She cooks mostly Italian cuisine and, as the Italians know the globe artichoke better than anyone, I knew she would have a good recipe. It's basic, but if you take the careful steps in preparation the taste will be out of this world.

Cleaning the artichoke is really important, and slightly tedious, but just do it.

Snap off the tough outer leaves of the artichoke by bending each one backwards (you can use scissors). Make sure you leave intact the soft little pillow of flavour on the inside of the leaf which is close to the heart.

Then slice off the top third of the globe so you can access the artichoke heart. You should now be able to stand the artichoke on their flat top.

Scrape out the centre of the heart where the little spiky or hairy part is. Peel off the rough outside of the stem. Now you should be able to eat every part of the artichoke.

Take a small handful of mint, a small handful of Italian parsley, half a clove of garlic and salt. Chop it together and bind it with a splash of olive oil.

Stuff the herb mixture into the hollowed-out centre and between the leaves of the artichoke.

Choose a frying pan with a thick base and a lid. Add enough olive oil to cover the bottom of the pan. Heat the oil over medium heat and stand the stuffed artichokes on their flat tops in the pan, and fry them for about 5 minutes. They should be almost caramelised, but don't burn them.

Now add enough hot water to cover the heart of the artichoke. Cover the pan and simmer on medium-low for about 10–15 minutes, until the artichoke can be pierced easily with a skewer.

Drain and serve on a plate. Drizzle with extra virgin olive oil and lemon wedges.

Serve as a vegetable side dish or as an entree, to be eaten with a knife and fork.

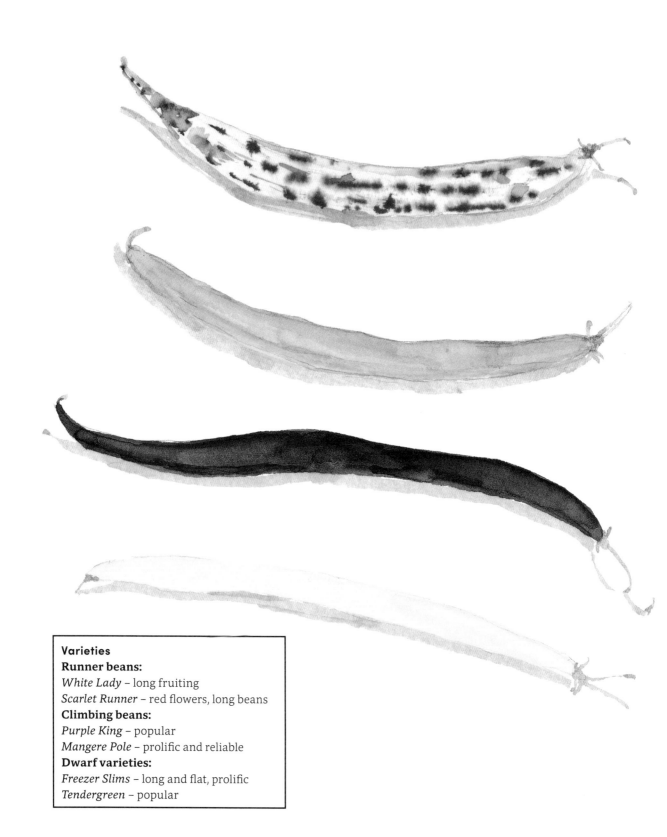

Varieties
Runner beans:
White Lady – long fruiting
Scarlet Runner – red flowers, long beans
Climbing beans:
Purple King – popular
Mangere Pole – prolific and reliable
Dwarf varieties:
Freezer Slims – long and flat, prolific
Tendergreen – popular

Beans

♈	**Sow** spring, summer
◎	**Harvest** summer, autumn
◷	**Growing time** 12–16 weeks
⚘⚘	**Space between plants** 20 cm
⊽	**Pots** yes
☼	**Aspect** full sun, part shade
⏚	**Soil pH** 6.8–7.5
❋	**Frost tolerant** no
♡	**Companions** carrots, celery, cucumber, chard, eggplant, corn, peas, potatoes, pumpkin, parsley, celeriac, lettuce, spinach
⌒	**Dislikes** beetroot, onions, chives

Sow

If you choose runner beans (perennial) they will die back in autumn and will return again in the springtime, so it is important to consider the planting site carefully. Prepare the soil well with compost and rotted manure (see p. 162). Sow beans directly into the ground 20 cm apart with a trellis or obelisk to grow on.

Seedlings can be started off early undercover at the end of winter (see p. 165). Plant out after the frosts have passed.

Nurture

Once flowering, keep your plants well watered and feed with a liquid fertiliser. Lack of water will cause the beans to drop. Keep a layer of mulch around the base of the plants to keep the soil moist.

Harvest

Once picking has started it is important to keep at it, picking every second day or so. Pick beans when they are young and tender. The more you pick the larger the crop.

Green bean and fried raisin salad

For 4

Blanch beans in a saucepan of boiling water and refresh in iced water. Dry on paper towel.

Make a dressing by whisking together the oil, lemon juice, honey and salt.

Heat an extra dash of oil in a small frying pan and fry the raisins until they plump up.

Toss the beans, rocket and raisins in the dressing and scatter almonds over the top.

2 large handfuls of green beans, trimmed
2 tbsp extra virgin olive oil
Juice of 1 lemon
1 tsp honey
½ tsp salt flakes
1 cup of raisins
1 large handful of rocket leaves
⅓ cup almonds, toasted and coarsely chopped

Bok choy and pak choy

♈ **Sow** spring, summer, autumn

◎ **Harvest** all year

◔ **Growing time** 6–8 weeks

♈♈ **Space between plants** 10 cm

🪴 **Pots** yes

☀ **Aspect** full sun

⊥ **Soil pH** 5.8–7.0

❋ **Frost tolerant** yes

♡ **Companions** beans, beetroot, onions, carrots, peas, potatoes

◔ **Dislikes** cauliflower, Brussels sprouts

Varieties
Red Purple – purple in colour, tangy sweet
Choi Green – thick round leaves, can be eaten raw or cooked
White Baby Stem – compact, thick white stem

Sow
Seedlings can be started off undercover in seed trays (see p. 165). Seeds should be sown 1 cm deep and thinned out to small pots at 5 cm. Seeds can also be directly sown into their beds after soil preparation (see p. 158). Use a high-nitrogen fertiliser such as chicken manure. Create drills (shallow lines in the soil made with a pointed stick or dibber) in rows at 30 cm intervals to the depth of 1 cm. Sprinkle seeds at 5 cm apart and as they grow thin the plants to 10 cm apart.

Nurture
Liquid feed every two weeks or so. Keep the plants well watered in the hotter months.

Harvest
Plants can be harvested from when the plant is young through to maturity. Snip stems near the base to allow for regrowth.

Stir-fried bok choy

For 4

Someone I know posted on social media that they were declaring their dislike for bok choy. WHAT! It's easy to grow and seriously delicious when cooked very simply.

Wash the bok choy and slice each one lengthways into quarters.

Heat the oil in a wok, fry the ginger and garlic for 1 minute then add the bok choy. Stir fry for about 5 minutes, until glossy and soft. Sprinkle with chilli (if using).

4 bok choy
2 tbsp peanut oil or avocado oil
2 tsp finely grated ginger
2 garlic cloves, crushed
1 long red chilli, deseeded and finely chopped (optional)

Cape gooseberry

🜨 **Sow** mid-spring to midsummer

◎ **Harvest** summer, autumn

🕐 **Growing time** 16–20 weeks

🛎 **Space between plants** 50 cm

🗑 **Pots** possible

☀ **Aspect** sunny, part shade

⚖ **Soil pH** 5.5–7.5

❄ **Frost tolerant** no

♡ **Companions** basil, asparagus, carrots, chives, nasturtiums parsnips, borage, marigolds

☺ **Dislikes** rosemary, dill, potatoes, kohlrabi, fennel, strawberries

Varieties

Golden Nugget – large sweet fruit
Giallo Grosso – best eaten raw
New Sugar Giant – large size bush

Sow

Depending on where you live the cape gooseberry can either be an annual or perennial. They don't tolerate frost so if you are in a frost-prone area they will be annuals. Seeds can be started undercover in a warm spot in seed trays in late winter to be planted out after frosts (see p. 165). For direct planting, prepare your soil (see p. 158). Sow seeds 4 mm deep and sow more than you need; thin to the healthiest plants after a few weeks of growth, leaving 50 cm between plants. The seeds can be slow to germinate (2–4 weeks).

Nurture

If your plants aren't thriving, fertilise with a complete organic fertiliser; however, the cape gooseberry usually needs very little attention.

Harvest

Fruit usually is ripe 16–20 weeks from planting. The fruit is ripe when the husk around the berry dries out and goes papery and pale. If the fruit is a bit green, leave it on a windowsill till the berry is a deep golden colour.

CAPE

GOOSEBERRY

Cape gooseberry and amaretti fool

For 6

Remove the gooseberries from their casings. Place gooseberries and sugar in a saucepan and break up the fruit with a wooden spoon as they come to a boil. Once they become syrupy set aside to cool and refrigerate till cold.

Whip the cream and icing sugar until it sits in soft folds. Fold in half of the chilled fruit then scatter the remaining fruit throughout as you decant it into your individual dishes. Top with extra gooseberries and crushed amaretti biscuits to serve.

500 g cape gooseberries, plus 6 extra to serve
½ cup sugar
310 ml (1¼ cups) whipping cream
3 tbsp icing sugar, to taste
6 amaretti biscuits, crushed

CAPE GOOSEBERRY FOOL

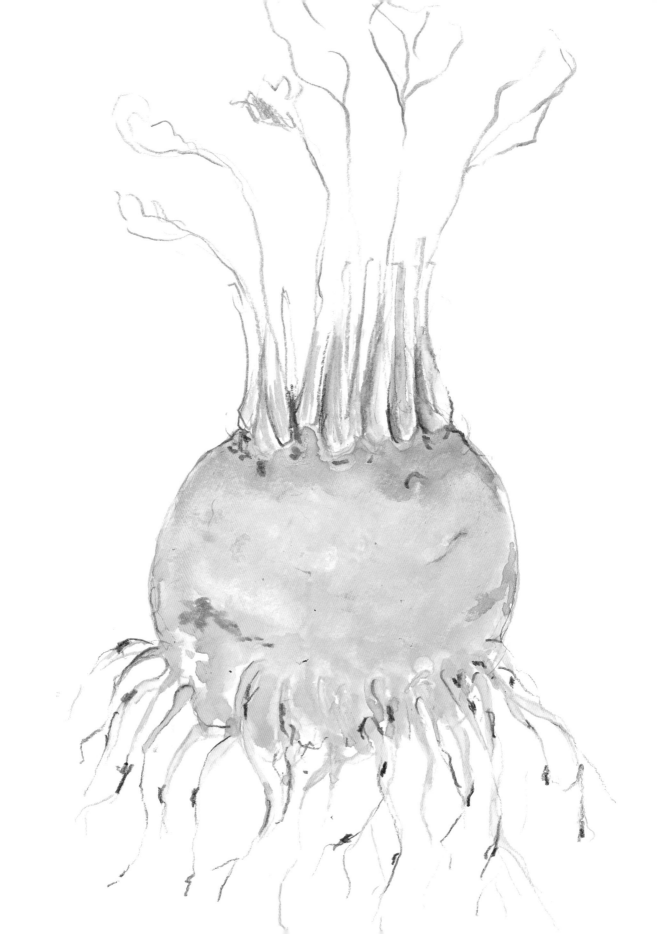

Celeriac

⚘	**Sow** spring, summer
◎	**Harvest** autumn, winter
◷	**Growing time** 30 weeks
⚘⚘	**Space between plants** 30 cm
⛉	**Pots** possible
☼	**Aspect** full sun, part shade
⬇	**Soil pH** 6.8–7.5
❄	**Frost tolerant** yes
♡	**Companions** beans, garlic, leeks, onions
◌	**Dislikes** carrots, corn, parsnips, potatoes, lettuce

Varieties

Prague Giant – creamy texture, less likely to bolt
Verona – slow grower
White Alabaster – popular, good flavour

Sow

Start seed off in late spring or early summer to avoid the plants bolting to seed. Sow seed 1 cm deep into trays and use heat mats to move them along. They are ready to plant out when the seedlings are large enough to handle.

Prepare the soil (see p. 158). It's best to plant seedlings at least 30 cm apart.

Nurture

Celeriac is a tolerant plant and reasonably easy to grow. As the plant becomes bigger, remove some of the outer leaves so that the crown is exposed. Feed with liquid fertiliser every now and then and keep well watered.

Harvest

Celeriac can be harvested from autumn or when they are the size of a tennis ball. The smaller roots are good eaten raw in salads, larger ones are good for roasting and soups. They might need some loosening of the soil with a garden fork to lift them.

Celeriac and prosciutto remoulade

My cousin Melly Beilby, who owns the catering company Spoonful, has had this delicious canapé on her menu for years, that's because it's so good!

Peel and finely julienne a celeriac bulb and put the flesh in a bowl of water and lemon juice. Prepare a homemade mayonnaise (careful to not over-salt) or use a ready-made one. Drain the celeriac and dry on a kitchen towel. Mix with enough mayonnaise to help it stick together. Lay out slices of prosciutto, place a spoonful of mixture at one end and roll up into neat little bite-sized packages and secure with a toothpick.

Celery

♈	**Sow** spring, summer
◎	**Harvest** summer, autumn, winter
◷	**Growing time** 18 weeks
❦❦	**Space between plants** 30 cm
⊽	**Pots** no
☀	**Aspect** full sun
⏚	**Soil pH** 6.8–7.5
✳	**Frost tolerant** yes
♡	**Companions** everything except those listed below
⊘	**Dislikes** carrots, corn, parsnips, potatoes, lettuce

Sow

Seedlings can be bought from garden centres or started as seed in trays in the greenhouse (see p. 165). Germination can be slow, so I tend to buy seedlings to plant in early summer. Plant out at about 10 cm tall into well prepared soil (see p. 158).

Nurture

Use extra compost and mulch around the plants to retain the moisture in the soil. Celery is best when watered regularly with a timer watering system. Celery that hasn't been well watered will be stringy and bitter. Some varieties will need their stalks wrapped (usually just in newspaper) while they are growing to prevent stringy or bitter celery. This is called blanching; however, some varieties are self-blanching. Liquid fertiliser is also very important, every two weeks. The small seedlings are a slug's salad, so keep the creatures at bay by distracting them into a pub crawl with partially buried paper cups half-filled with beer. Bye slugs! (See p. 186.)

Harvest

To harvest, pick off the outside stems by pulling them off at ground level, or slice off the whole plant at the roots and watch it regrow.

Celery, celeriac, egg, parsley and capers salad

For 6–8 as a side dish

Peel the celeriac then slice thinly (2–3 mm), then slice again into strips to make matchsticks about 5 cm in length. To prevent your cut celeriac from browning, submerge it in a bowl of water with lemon before mixing. In a serving bowl, combine the celeriac with the other salad ingredients.

Whisk the salad dressing together and toss it through the salad, making sure everything is well covered. Garnish with walnuts and eggs scattered on top. Serve on top of sliced crusty bread, if you wish. Flaked or poached salmon can be added if you wish to make this recipe a main rather than a side dish.

1 celeriac
1½ cups celery stalks, thinly sliced
1 cup flat-leaf parsley, chopped
⅓ cup capers, rinsed and drained
1 cup chopped walnuts, to garnish
7 hard-boiled eggs, halved, to garnish
Crusty bread, to serve (optional)

Dressing
80 ml (⅓ cup) white wine vinegar or lemon juice
2 tsp Dijon mustard
80 ml (⅓ cup) extra virgin olive oil
85 g (⅓ cup) whole egg mayonnaise

Varieties
Stringless – popular, likes water
Green Crunch – self-blanching and
    good flavour
Vert d'Elne – popular

BOIL GRILL MILL

Varieties
Honey 'n Pearl – white and yellow kernels
Early Chief – large cob and very sweet
Honeysweet – easy to grow
Sun 'n' Snow – good flavour and easy to grow
Xtra-Tender – early to harvest

Corn

♈	**Sow** spring, summer
◎	**Harvest** summer, autumn
◷	**Growing time** 14 weeks
⚥	**Space between plants** 30 cm
⛉	**Pots** yes (large)
☀	**Aspect** full sun
⊥	**Soil pH** 5.8–7.0
✳	**Frost tolerant** no
♡	**Companions** beans, zucchini, cucumbers, pumpkins
⊙	**Dislikes** tomatoes, celery, celeriac

Sow
Can be started off in the greenhouse to be planted out after the frosts or when they are about 10 cm tall. After frosts, sow directly into very well-prepared soil (see p. 158) with lots of compost, manure and mulch. Plant 30 cm apart, in a block to help them support each other and prevent toppling over. Corn must be planted en masse to ensure effective pollination.

Nurture
Corn doesn't need staking; in fact, it can act as a stake for other climbers such as beans or cucumbers. Famously planted together are the 'three sisters': corn, beans and zucchini. All benefit each other in their growth, so they are the ultimate in companion planting. Corn needs lots of water so keep it up to them.

Harvest
Corn is ready after 14 weeks from planting out or 6 weeks from flowering. When the corncobs start angling out at a right angle and the tassels on the ends of the cobs are starting to brown, they are ready. Twist off the corncobs or cut off with a knife.

Polenta

Polenta is simply made by grinding dried corn in a grinder or high-speed blender. Homemade polenta is creamier than store-bought, so it's worth a try. You will need to dry your corn in a dehydrator or your oven.

If using a dehydrator, cut the corn kernels from the cobs and spread them on the dehydrator trays in a single layer. Dehydrate for 8 hours.

If using an oven, set the oven on its lowest heat (usually about 50–90°C). Spread corn kernels on a baking tray lined with baking paper, leave the oven door ajar and cook for 8–10 hours. The corn kernels need to be hard and brittle.

To make polenta, put the dried kernels into your grinder or blender and whiz until you have a very fine cornmeal. To cook, simmer 1 cup polenta in 4 cups milk, water or chicken stock, stirring constantly with a whisk, for about 40 minutes until all liquid is absorbed. Turn off the heat and add 30 g of butter and half a cup of parmesan cheese. Stir through and serve.

Cucumber

♈	**Sow** spring, summer
◎	**Harvest** summer, autumn
◷	**Growing time** 16–20 weeks
⚊⚊	**Space between plants** 30 cm
⛉	**Pots** yes
☀	**Aspect** full sun, part shade
⇧	**Soil pH** 6.8–7.5
✱	**Frost tolerant** yes
♡	**Companions** everything except those listed below
⌣	**Dislikes** potatoes, tomatoes, sage

Varieties
Green Gem – small prickles, mild flavour
Lebanese – long, firm, great flavour
Continental – extra long, sweet
Apple – white skin, round
Burpless – popular, long, grow on trellis
Mouse melon or *cucamelon* – tiny grape-sized fruit with a skin that looks like a melon

Sow
Germinate seed undercover (see p. 166) in late winter to plant out after frosts. Cucumbers do well with a heat mat. Cultivate the soil with manure and compost. Plant out seedlings or seeds when the weather is warm. Choose a sunny spot beside a trellis or three stakes wound with twine. There should be a spacing between plants of 30 cm. Plant flowers such as nasturtiums and borage nearby to attract bees, as this will help with pollination.

Nurture
Cucumbers have a very high water content and therefore watering is very important. Water the plants low to the ground to prevent fungal diseases. They do well with a commercial tomato fertiliser, used according to the manufacturer's instructions. Cucumbers are gross feeders, so regular applications of fertiliser are needed.

Harvest
As soon as the fruit is the right size, use scissors to remove. It's important that the fruit is regularly picked and not left on the vine too long. Younger fruit can be used to pickle as gherkins.

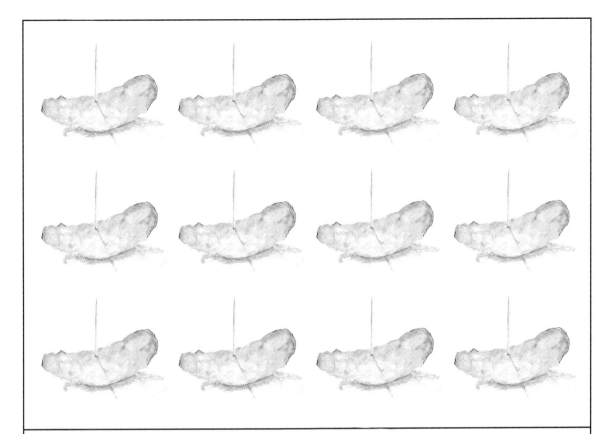

Bread and butter pickles

Makes 1 large or 2 small preserving jars

Combine the cucumber, onion and salt into a non-reactive bowl. Place in the fridge overnight to soften. When ready drain, rinse and pat dry the mix with paper towel.

Place the vinegar, sugar, mustard and coriander seeds into a large saucepan on medium heat and cook for 5 minutes. Add the onion, cucumber and turmeric and bring to a simmer, then remove from heat.

Transfer into sterilised jars (see p. 190), add a bay leaf to each jar and seal with clean lids. Use the canning method of submerging the filled and sealed jars in a large pot of water that covers the jars completely. Boil for 15 minutes, carefully remove the jars and stand them on a wooden chopping board to cool. This will help prevent your pickles from spoiling.

The jars are best stored in the fridge, but can be stored unopened in a cool pantry for 3 months.

5 cucumbers, thinly sliced (Lebanese are good for this)
1 large brown onion, thinly sliced
1 tbsp salt
375 ml (1½ cups) apple cider vinegar
1 cup caster sugar
2 tsp mustard seeds
2 tsp coriander seeds
1 tsp turmeric powder
2 bay leaves

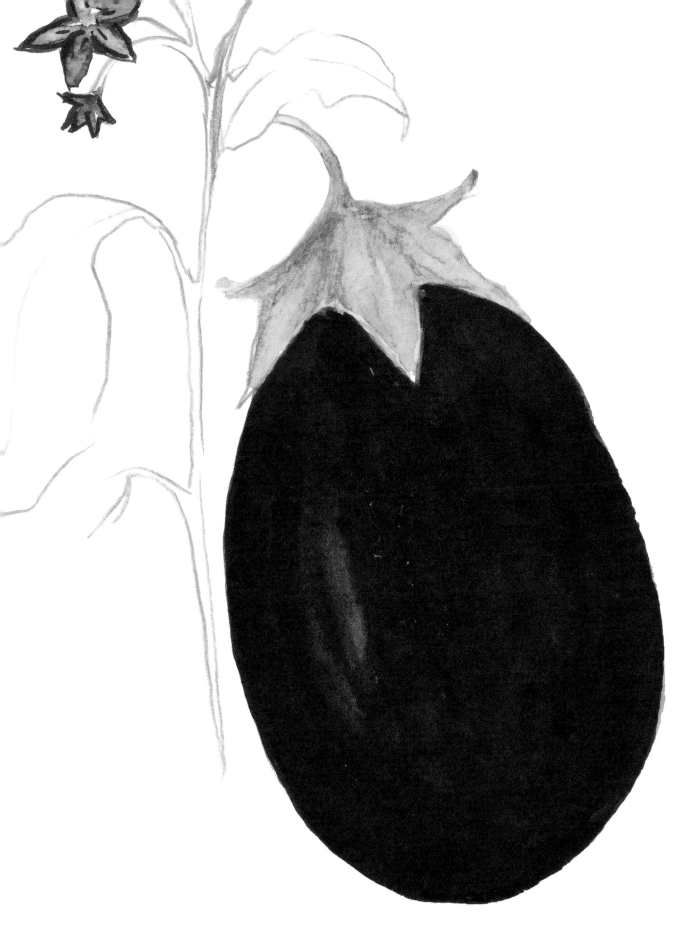

Eggplant

♈	**Sow** mid-spring to midsummer
◎	**Harvest** late summer, autumn
◷	**Growing time** 16 weeks
♈♈	**Space between plants** 60 cm
▽	**Pots** yes
☼	**Aspect** full sun
⊥	**Soil pH** 4.5–5.8
✳	**Frost tolerant** no
♡	**Companions** potatoes, peas, beans, capsicums, tomatoes
◠	**Dislikes** bok choy, brassicas

Varieties
Moneymaker – prolific
Blacknite – reliable
Early Long Purple – good for moussaka
Listada di Gandia – speckled
Lebanese – long thin fruit, such as *Long Purple* or *Midnight*

Sow
Start seeds in early spring or even undercover in winter to be more advanced. Sow seeds into prepared seedling trays with seed-raising mix and water. Keep watered and in a warm spot (a heat mat can be used). They should be moist and not waterlogged. Liquid feed once a week.

They can be bought as seedlings. Four plants will yield a good amount of fruit for the average-sized family. The earlier you get eggplants underway, the better success you will have so aim for advanced seedlings at the point of planting. To plant out, prepare the soil well with compost, rotted manure and a mulch topping. Plant out after frosts (mid to late spring or earlier in frost-free zones) into the sunniest part of the garden, when the seedling is looking strong and roots are escaping from the bottom of the seedling pod. Space plants 60 cm apart.

Nurture
Eggplants need staking and this is best done early so that the plant's roots aren't damaged. A single stake is suitable. Keep the central stem of the plant securely attached to the stake as the fruit tends to be heavy and can pull the plant over. Watering is important: don't let the plant dry out. Once flowers have appeared, switch from a weekly liquid feed to a fertiliser with a high potash content. This will enhance the flowering and therefore the fruiting. Pinch out the tips of the plant to encourage side branching: 4 to 6 branches are good.

Harvest
Harvest when the fruit's skin is smooth, dark in colour, shiny and the eggplants are the right size. Cut off the stem rather than pulling the fruit off. Pick regularly and refrigerate after picking until ready for use. Freshly picked young eggplants rarely need salting as the bitterness is usually only present in older fruit.

Imam baldi (stuffed eggplants)

For 12 as a starter or side dish

Recipe by Kathy Tsaples

This recipe is from my dear friend, Kathy Tsaples. She is the author of the Sweet Greek *cookbooks and her recipes are wonderful and well-worth trying. This recipe is perfect for a long lunch of grazing, ideally under a apple tree with lots of good wine and crusty bread.*

....

Cut the tops off the eggplants and slice down the middle lengthwise. This will enable you to scoop out the flesh using a spoon. Take your time and be careful. Finely chop up the flesh and sauté it in a pan.

In a bowl, combine your chopped tomatoes, spring onions, parsley, mint, onions, garlic, salt, pepper, tomato paste and half a cup of olive oil, creating a divine and aromatic mixture. Add the sautéed eggplant flesh.

Lay the eggplant shells in a baking dish. Spoon in the mixture until the shells are filled up. Any remaining mixture should be spooned around the eggplant.

Drizzle over the remaining cup of olive oil and bake in an oven set to a moderate temperature for an hour.

If the eggplants are browning too quickly, cover them with foil.

6 medium eggplants

3–4 ripe tomatoes, roughly chopped

1 bunch of spring onions, roughly chopped

1 bunch of parsley, finely chopped

1 small bunch of mint, finely chopped

3 brown onions, sliced

10 cloves of garlic, finely chopped

Salt and pepper

1 tbsp tomato paste

1½ cup olive oil

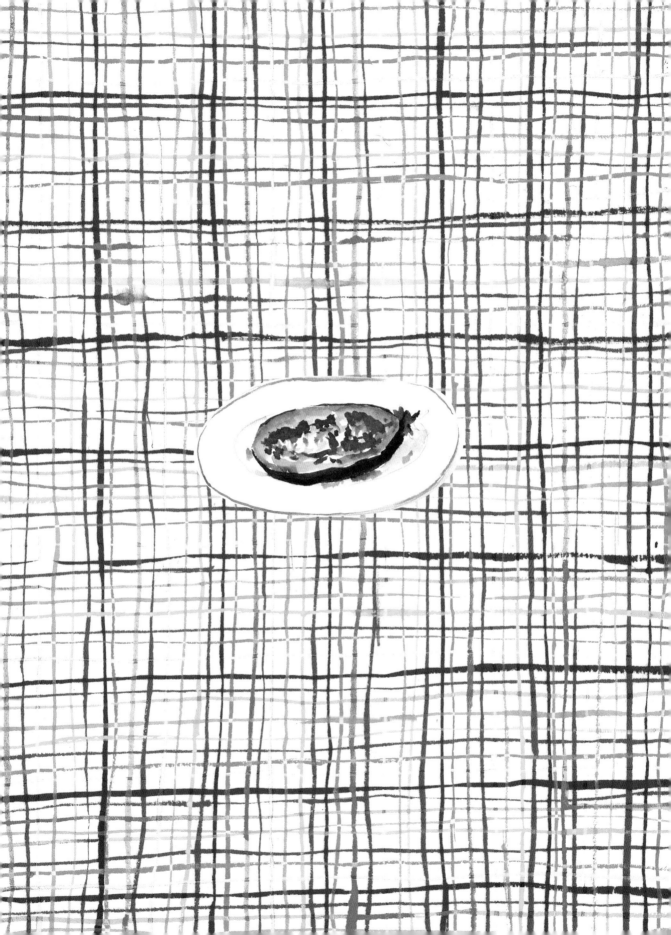

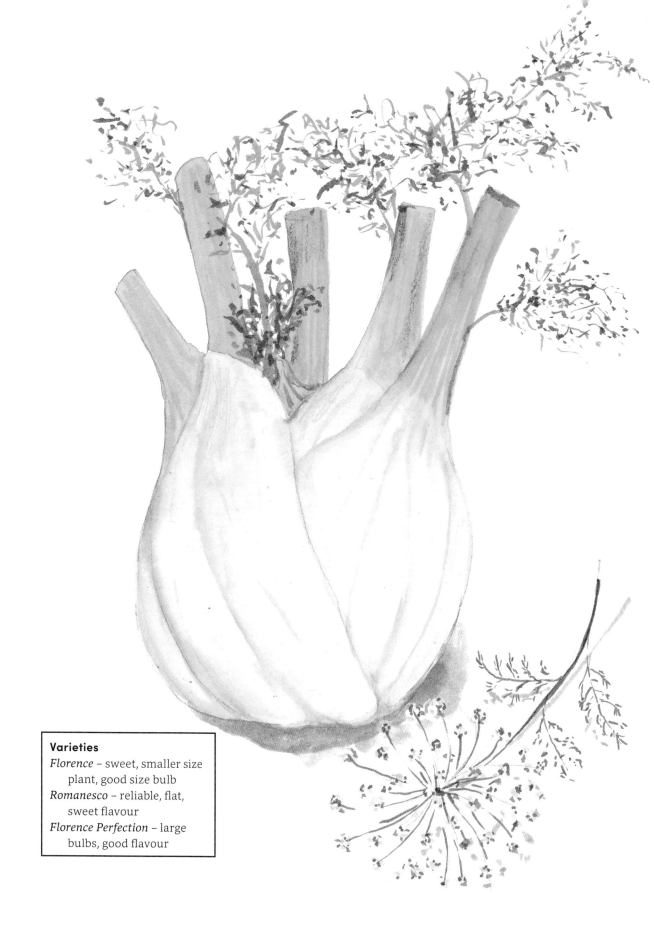

Fennel

♈	**Sow** spring, summer, autumn
◎	**Harvest** autumn, winter, spring
☉	**Growing time** 12–22 weeks
♈♈	**Space between plants** 30 cm
⛁	**Pots** possible
☀	**Aspect** full sun
⎊	**Soil pH** 6.8–7.5
✳	**Frost tolerant** yes
♡	**Companions** basil, dill
◌	**Dislikes** beans, broad beans, capsicums, tomatoes, coriander, eggplant

Sow
Prepare your soil with well-rotted manure and compost (see p. 159). Sow seeds directly into the garden bed in spring and summer. The planting depth is 2.5 cm and is best in rows. Thin out if overcrowded. Each plant needs about 30 cm of space and produces one bulb. You can start your seedlings off undercover if need be (see p. 166).

Nurture
Keep the plants well-watered. Liquid feed regularly. Pile the soil (this is called earthing up) around the bulb of each plant to blanch, making its flavour sweeter.

Harvest
With some varieties you can harvest when it reaches your preferred size: the florence variety is a good example, where the bulb can be large or small depending on how you might want to use it. The plant takes about 3–5 months to mature. Bulbs are pulled out whole, or you can slice them off at the base for a regrowth.

Insalata di arance e finocchi

For 8

Adapted from Frank Fariello's recipe

Use a mandolin or thinly slice the fennel trying to keep the floral shape by halving the bulbs from top to bottom and taking slices from the cut side.

Use a sharp knife to peel the oranges by first cutting off the top and bottom and sitting the fruit on its cut end. Then slice the peel off with downward strokes, removing the pith layer as well. Hold the peeled orange in your hand and remove the segments by cutting either side of the pith that divides the segments. Each segment should now be pith-less.

Layer the orange, fennel and onion (if using) on a platter and scatter with the olives and fennel fronds. Season with flaky salt and pepper and drizzle with the olive oil.

3–4 smallish fennel bulbs, fronds reserved

4–5 oranges

½ red onion, thinly sliced (optional)

Handful of black olives, dried ones or kalamata

Flaky salt and coarsely ground black pepper

Extra virgin olive oil, for dressing

Horseradish

⚘	**Sow** mid-spring after frost
◎	**Harvest** autumn, winter, spring
◷	**Growing time** 8 weeks
⚏	**Space between plants** 50 cm
⬯	**Pots** yes
☀	**Aspect** full sun
⇂	**Soil pH** 5.5–7.5
✳	**Frost tolerant** no
♡	**Companions** potatoes, sweet potatoes, strawberries, rhubarb
⊙	**Dislikes** none

Varieties
Common or *Maliner Kren* – can be vulnerable to diseases
Bohemian Giant – more resistant to disease
Variegata – has a creamy texture and lovely variegated leaves

Sow
Horseradish is easy to grow; in fact, it can completely take over so it is a good idea to plant in a big pot. Choose a sunny spot and prepare the soil well. Bury 15 cm long roots 50 cm apart.

Nurture
Horseradish is so easy to grow that it doesn't usually need any care other than planting and watering. Just be mindful that it grows quickly and can be invasive. To prevent this, you can cut out the bottom of a largish black tub and bury it so it surrounds your plants.

Harvest
Harvest after the first frosts or late autumn. Dig deep and loosen soil with a garden fork, then pull up the whole plant. Both the roots and the leaves are edible.

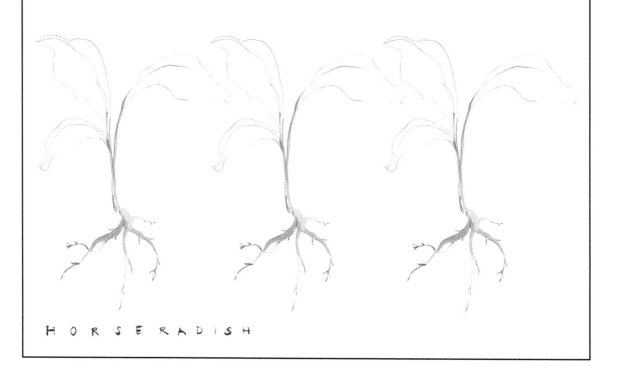

HORSERADISH

SARDINES WITH SORREL, PICKLED ONION & HORSERADISH AIOLI ON TOAST

Sardines on toast with sorrel and horseradish aioli

For 4

Poach the onion for a few minutes in a small saucepan with the red wine vinegar and sugar, then set aside to cool.

Brush the bread with olive oil and grill until the bread is well toasted. Meanwhile, combine the horseradish and aioli in a small bowl.

Lay the toast on serving plates and spread with horseradish aioli. Top with sardines, onion and sorrel leaves. Squeeze lemon juice over and drizzle with olive oil. Season with salt and pepper.

½ cup red onion, thinly sliced

250ml (1 cup) red wine vinegar

2 tsp sugar, or to taste

4 slices of thick sourdough bread

Extra virgin olive oil

1–2 tsp finely grated fresh horseradish

4 tbsp aioli

12 sardines, fresh and pan fried or tinned (the best quality you can find)

Small sorrel leaves, to serve

1 lemon, to squeeze over

Salt and pepper

Jerusalem artichokes

🌱 **Sow** spring, summer

◎ **Harvest** autumn, winter

🕐 **Growing time** 30–36 weeks

🌱 **Space between plants** 30 cm

🪣 **Pots** no

☀ **Aspect** full sun

⎁ **Soil pH** 6.8–7.5

❄ **Frost tolerant** yes

♡ **Companions** everything except those listed below

☹ **Dislikes** beans, garlic, potatoes, tomatoes, onions, leeks, chives

Varieties
Wild White – great flavour and has a good yield
Wild Red – smallish tubers that grow faster than other varieties
Stampede – very vigorous and can spread easily

Sow
Source tubers from a friend or garden centre. Prepare your soil (see p. 158) with compost and well-rotted manure. Bury tubers to the depth of 15 cm at 30 cm apart. The new shoots will grow quickly in springtime and will need protecting from slugs and snails.

Nurture
When the shoots are 30 cm high, build up the soil around the stems. This will help support the plants. Keep well watered and weed free. Plants can be held upright by being staked as a group. Use stakes and twine and fence them in. The plant will produce flowers that should be pinched out so that energy is diverted into the tubers. When the leaves start turning yellow, the plant will be sending its nutrients down to its tubers. Cut down to 30 cm when the leaves start dropping.

Harvest
Harvest as you need as the tubers don't store very well. Tubers that are left in the ground will reshoot next year.

Jerusalem artichoke soup with crisps

For 6

Gently cook the leeks (in a heavy bottomed saucepan) in olive oil and butter until soft and creamy.

Chop up the kilo of Jerusalem artichokes and add to the leeks. Pour in the stock and boil until the artichokes are very soft. If you have a stick blender, wizz it up until it's smooth. Add in the cream and salt.

Heat the vegetable oil in a small saucepan or deep fryer. Thinly slice the extra artichokes into discs with a mandolin. Pat dry and when the oil is very hot (test by dropping one in, it should rapidly boil around the chip). In small batches drop the discs into the oil until brown and crisp.

Serve soup with the crisps and pan-fried sage leaves (if using) on top.

2 leeks (white part only), sliced

2 tbsp olive oil

50 g butter

1 kilo of Jerusalem artichokes plus ½ kilo for crisps

5 cups of chicken stock (or vegetable)

250 ml pouring cream

1 tsp flaky salt

Vegetable oil for deep frying

Pan-fried sage leaves, to serve (optional)

Leeks

♈	**Sow** spring, summer
◎	**Harvest** autumn, winter
◔	**Growing time** 30–32 weeks
♥♥	**Space between plants** 15 cm
⊽	**Pots** possible
☼	**Aspect** full sun
⏚	**Soil pH** 6.8–7.5
❋	**Frost tolerant** yes
♡	**Companions** everything except those listed below
⊙	**Dislikes** beans, broad beans, peas, artichokes

Varieties

Autumn Giant – long, good size and flavour
Mammoth Blanch – mild, good harvest as baby leeks
Musselburgh – popular and reliable

Sow

Sprinkle seeds into prepared seedling mix trays and cover with vermiculite grains to help keep moist. Keep watered with a spray bottle. When they have reached the height of 10 cm or so they can be planted out at 15 cm intervals in the vegetable patch. Use a dibber to create a deep hole of 12 cm. Trim the roots to 2.5 cm and drop a plant into each hole and bury it. Water in well.

You can also sow directly in late spring or early summer into well-fertilised and prepared soil with good drainage (see p. 158). Sprinkle seeds in situ and thin out as necessary. When they are about 10 cm, plant out into deep holes spaced at 20 cm.

Nurture

As the plant grows, pile the dirt up the side of the leeks. This is called earthing up and will help to encourage growth of the white part of the leek. Liquid feed fortnightly.

Harvest

Harvest when stems are about 2 cm diameter. Leeks will often need a garden fork to lift. It is best to harvest in the autumn and winter, as in spring they tend to develop a tough flower stem.

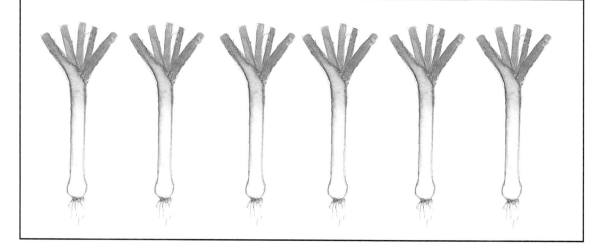

Chicken and leek pie

For 4–6

This is not an earth-shatteringly exciting dish, but a total winner in the comfort food stakes. My children's friends used to beg me for these pies. I like to serve them with a lemony, zesty rocket salad.

....

Preheat the oven to 210°C.

Chop the chicken into bite-size pieces.

Melt the extra butter in a frying pan and fry the leeks until soft. Add the chicken and fry until it changes colour, but don't brown it.

Gently poach the chicken and leeks in the milk for 5 minutes. Drain, reserving the milk.

Melt the butter in a medium saucepan. Add the flour and cook for a minute or two. Gradually add the reserved milk, stirring until you have a thick white sauce. Add the chicken mixture, mustard, tarragon and the cream and stir to combine. Set aside to cool while you prepare the pastry.

At this stage you can either make four individual pies or one family pie. Line a greased pie dish or dishes with pastry, fill with pastry weights or uncooked rice and blind bake for 10 minutes. Remove from the oven and fill with the chicken mixture. Place pastry on top, trim to size and brush with the beaten egg. Bake for 20 minutes or until golden brown.

400 g mix of chicken breast and thigh fillets

2 leeks, washed and finely chopped

50 g butter, plus 20 g extra, for frying

1 litre (4 cups) of milk

⅓ cup plain flour

1 tsp Dijon mustard

½ cup chopped tarragon

150 ml pure cream

Fresh or frozen puff pastry (enough for a family pie dish or four individual pies)

1 egg, beaten

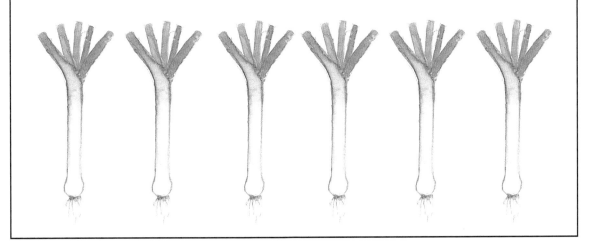

Parsnip

♈	**Sow** spring, summer
◎	**Harvest** summer, autumn, winter
◔	**Growing time** 32–36 weeks
♈♈	**Space between plants** 20–30 cm
⛻	**Pots** possible
☼	**Aspect** full sun
⌻	**Soil pH** 6.8–7.5
✳	**Frost tolerant** yes
♡	**Companions** most things, except those listed below
☉	**Dislikes** carrots, celery, celeriac

Varieties

Gladiators – popular, long hybrid
Yatesnip – smooth skin, high yields
VIP – good for a home garden

Sow

Parsnips are best sown directly. Prepare the soil (see p. 158), paying particular attention to creating a loose soil with lots of compost. The soil needs to be free of stones, as they will disturb the root's development. Manure added to the soil must be well rotted to ensure the parsnip root doesn't become scorched.

Sow the seeds 2 cm deep, 10 cm apart. The soil needs to be moist before planting and kept moist during germination. The seedling bed can be covered with frost cloth or hessian sacking. Remove the cover once the seedlings appear. Germination can take up to 20 days. Thin seedlings to avoid overcrowding by selecting the strongest plants. Spacing should be 20–30 cm.

Nurture

Water plants evenly to help them create healthy roots. Plants that are left to dry out will fail to thrive and uneven watering will cause them to split. Liquid feed the plants to encourage resilience and growth. Aphids love parsnip seedlings so watch out for them. If they come under attack use an aphid spray (see p. 187).

Harvest

Parsnips are best harvested in the cooler weather when they will develop a sweeter flavour; the cold converts the starches in the root into sugar for a sweeter parsnip. Use a garden fork to loosen the soil for harvest. Parsnips can be left in the ground and used as needed or pulled up and stored in a cool dark place. Keep a couple of plants in the ground to bolt to seed so you can gather it for next year's planting.

Warm winter salad of parsnips, feta and orange

For 6–8

My cousin Jim was a bit down and I said, 'I hope you're okay?' He replied, 'Nothing a tub of Dodoni feta won't fix.' So this one is for you, Jim.

....

Preheat the oven to 200°C.

Peel and then quarter the parsnips lengthwise. If they are particularly long, halve them in length. Lay the parsnip and onion on a baking tray sprinkled with chopped rosemary and salt. Drizzle with olive oil and rub it into the vegetables. Roast for 25–30 minutes, turning the parsnips a couple of times. Once the onion is soft and the parsnip is golden, add the walnuts and roast for a further 7 minutes. Remove from the oven and set aside to cool.

Meanwhile, whisk together the dressing ingredients.

On a large plate scatter the witlof leaves and drizzle with half the dressing. Toss well to completely cover the leaves. Gently layer the salad with the onion and parsnip and the orange. Pour the rest of the dressing over and scatter with chunks of feta. Nice with grilled meats.

6 parsnips

1 red onion, cut into wedges

2 rosemary sprigs, leaves picked and chopped

2 good pinches of flaky salt

Olive oil, for drizzling

1 cup chopped walnut (big chunks)

3 red witlof (chicory), leaves separated (you can substitute radicchio)

1 large orange, peeled and thinly sliced

150 g Greek-style feta (such as Dodoni)

Dressing

4 tbsp extra virgin olive oil

2 tsp Dijon mustard

80 ml (⅓ cup) red wine vinegar

1 tbsp honey

Passionfruit

♈	**Sow** spring, summer	
◎	**Harvest** spring, summer	
⚏	**Space between plants** 1.5 m	
◷	**Growing time until fruit** 12–18 months	
⊽	**Pots** yes	
☼	**Aspect** full sun	
⬐	**Soil pH** 6.8–7.5	
✳	**Frost tolerant** light frosts only	
♡	**Companions** nasturtiums, marigolds for good pollination from bees	
☺	**Dislikes** none	

Varieties
Misty Gems – large yellow fruit that is less acidic than some
Sweetheart – black in colour and very sweet
Panama Red Pandora – self-pollinating, good flavour

Sow
Some varieties need another plant for cross-pollination, so check the planting label. Potted passionfruit plants are available from nurseries and garden centres and are best planted out in spring. The vine will need a trellis to grow on and they prefer an easterly aspect. Prepare the soil well (see p. 158) and cover the soil with plenty of mulch.

Nurture
Passionfruit requires moist soil and will need extra watering in summer. Add potash-rich fertiliser in spring. As the plant grows, tie in any stray outward-growing branches.

Harvest
Passionfruit will turn from green to purple–black when ripe. They should easily come off the vine when picked.

Passionfruit curd

Makes 1 medium preserving jar

Remove pulp from passionfruit and set aside. Discard the skins.

Beat the eggs, egg yolks and sugar together until pale and sugar has dissolved.

Melt the butter in a heavy–based saucepan on low heat. When butter is just melted, stir in the egg mixture and the passionfruit pulp and continue cooking gently, stirring constantly, until thickened.

Remove from the heat and set aside to cool slightly, then pour into a 350 ml (1½ cup) sterilised jar (see p. 190). Keep in the fridge for up to 3 weeks.

11 passionfruit
2 large eggs plus 2 large egg yolks
150 g (⅔ cup) caster sugar
100 g unsalted butter

Potatoes

♈	**Sow** spring
◎	**Harvest** summer, autumn, winter
◷	**Growing time** 12–22 weeks
♈♈	**Space between plants** 45–70 cm
⊽	**Pots** yes
☼	**Aspect** full sun
⚡	**Soil pH** 6.8–7.5
✳	**Frost tolerant** yes
♡	**Companions** everything except those listed below
⌢	**Dislikes** capsicums, carrots, celery, cucumbers, tomatoes, zucchini, apples, cherries, raspberries, strawberries, chillies, pumpkins, celeriac, spinach

Potatoes

1.	Coliban	**7.**	Nicola
2.	Desiree	**8.**	Dutch cream
3.	Chat	**9.**	Pink eye
4.	King Edward	**10.**	Purple congo
5.	Red pontiac	**11.**	Sweet potato
6.	Kipfler	**12.**	Sebago

Sow

Potatoes are grown from tubers known as seed potatoes. They are available from garden shops from midwinter until spring. Don't use sprouting potatoes bought from a supermarket. Seed potatoes are produced to deliver disease-free and flavoursome potatoes. The tubers are encouraged to sprout through a process called chitting. They are laid in a single layer in a box and placed in a dry, warm area away from direct sunlight. Under a verandah or in a shed is good.

Prepare soil with plenty of compost cultivated to 30 cm deep (see p. 159). Avoid fertiliser burn by making sure the manure is well rotted.

When the tubers have shoots approximately 5–10 cm long they are ready to plant.

Mark out rows 1 metre apart to the depth of 15 cm. Place the sprouted potato with the shoots facing up and bury. Water in well.

Potatoes do very well in containers (see growing in pots on p. 168).

Nurture

When the shoots break through the surface, mound up the soil halfway up the stems, and repeat the process 3 or 4 times before flowering. This will produce higher yields and prevent green potatoes.

Protect young plants from frost by using a frost sheet.

Keep soil moist but never waterlogged as this will cause rot. Once your plants are flowering, hold off on watering to reduce the risk of disease.

Use an all-purpose fertiliser and liquid feed if your plants aren't thriving.

Harvest

When you notice the flowers start to fade (in early summer) it is time to harvest the potatoes. A garden fork is a good way to loosen the soil, making access to the potatoes easier.

1.

2.

3.

4.

5.

6.

7.

8.

9.

10.

11.

12.

Tortilla de patatas

For 6

Preheat the oven to 200°C. Peel and slice the potatoes and onion very finely using a mandolin, if you have one.

Spread potato and onion on a baking tray and coat with a generous amount of oil (it should be swimming in oil … but don't worry, it gets drained off). Season with salt and pepper and bake until soft and just starting to caramelise. (This step can be done on the stove top, but I find it works well in the oven.) Remove from the oven (leave the oven on), and drain off any excess oil.

In a large bowl, lightly beat the eggs with a couple of good pinches of salt and freshly ground black pepper. Stir in the drained potato and onion. Set aside for 10 minutes.

Grease a heavy-based ovenproof frying pan and heat on high heat. Pour in the potato mixture and flatten the potatoes with a spatula until they're mostly even. Shake to encourage the batter to seep to the bottom of the pan. Cook the tortilla undisturbed for about 15 minutes until the top is not very runny but still wet, and it is golden underneath.

Transfer to the oven for 5 minutes to cook through.

Serve hot, cold or at room temperature. Slice into wedges and serve it plain, or with a dusting of smoked paprika and a squiggle of aioli or mayo.

3–4 waxy firm potatoes
1 small onion
250 ml (1 cup) olive oil
7 large eggs
Flaky salt and ground black pepper
Smoked paprika and aioli or
  mayonnaise, to serve

TORTILLA DE PATATAS

The Agrarian Kitchen's sourdough potato cakes

For 4

I recently did a cooking class at the famous Agrarian Kitchen Cooking School in Tasmania. Rodney Dunn and Séverine Demanet are so wonderfully knowledgeable on growing and cooking and their cooking school and restaurant is outstanding.

Heat oil in a large, deep saucepan or deep fryer to 160°C (when a cube of bread turns golden brown in 30 seconds). Meanwhile, wash 2 large pink eye potatoes and slice into 1 cm slices. Dust with flour. Thin some active sourdough starter with water until it is the consistency of pouring cream and dip each potato slice into the sourdough batter, then carefully lower the potato into the hot oil and fry until golden and crisp on the outside. Season with salt and pepper and serve.

Radishes

- ♈ **Sow** all year
- ◎ **Harvest** all year
- ◷ **Growing time** 5 weeks
- ♈♈ **Space between plants** 5–10 cm
- 🪴 **Pots** yes
- ☼ **Aspect** full sun
- ⚖ **Soil pH** 5.5–7.5
- ❋ **Frost tolerant** yes
- ♡ **Companions** beetroot, carrots, celery, silverbeet, potatoes, peas
- ⊙ **Dislikes** tomatoes, strawberries, capsicums, eggplant

Varieties
Cherry Belle – round
French Breakfast – long
Scarlet Globe – good fresh and roasted
Sparkler – peppery
Watermelon – pretty for salads

Sow
Prepare the bed with compost, manure and a layer of mulch.

Radishes are very easy to grow and seeds are best sprinkled directly into the garden bed.

They shouldn't be planted where brassicas have been growing, as the soil will be depleted of the right nutrients. Sow in succession to keep an endless supply as radishes don't store well once harvested.

Nurture
Keep watered: they are pretty self-sufficient and don't need much attention.

Harvest
Harvest as you need them. Try not to let them grow too big, as they become woody. Leave the odd one to produce flowers and seed pods for harvest. These can be collected once the pods are dried off.

Pan-fried radishes

For 6 as a side dish

Warm a pan over medium heat and add the butter. When the butter is foaming and starting to turn nut brown, add the radishes, tossing constantly. Cook for 10–15 minutes until soft and glossy. Pile into a serving dish, squeeze lemon juice over and sprinkle with flaky salt.

100 g butter
500 g radishes, leaves removed, halved
Juice of ½ a lemon
Flaky salt

RADISH

- SAUTÉ

- PICKLE
- ROAST
- SLICE

RADISH FLOWER

- EDIBLE

- PICKLE

- SALAD

Rhubarb

♈	**Sow** spring
◎	**Harvest** spring, summer, autumn
◷	**Growing time** 12–25 months
♈♈	**Space between plants** 1 m
⊽	**Pots** no
☀	**Aspect** full sun
⏚	**Soil pH** 6.8–7.5
✳	**Frost tolerant** yes
♡	**Companions** most things
⌒	**Dislikes** none

Varieties

Ruby Red Dwarf – sweet sharp flavour
Silvan Giant – good in cool climates
Victoria – popular, good yield and sweet

Sow

Rhubarb prefers a cool climate. The soil needs to be well worked before planting (see p. 158).

Buy crowns or gather them from a fellow gardener. Divide the crown using a sharp clean spade and plant 1 metre apart with the buds just below the soil level.

Nurture

Keep your rhubarb well watered. The plant needs a year to establish itself and shouldn't be harvested in the first year. Cut the rhubarb flowers off when they appear and feed with liquid fertiliser to promote more stalks. Keep the plants mulched to retain moisture, as drying out will create thin stems. You can 'force' rhubarb in winter by using an upturned bucket or special terracotta rhubarb forcer pot. This creates a microclimate that forces the stems out of the ground so they are ready to harvest in a couple of weeks. This is only suitable for the first couple of weeks, then you need to remove it for the rest of the season. Forced rhubarb tends to be sweeter and more tender.

Harvest

Resist the temptation to harvest your rhubarb in the first year as it develops as this will help the plant establish itself. When it's ready, pull or twist the stalks with a firm outwards action. The stalks can be pulled at any thickness but always from the outside of the plant. The leaf part of the plant is toxic, but it can be composted. Don't feed the leaves to chickens or other animals.

RHUBARB

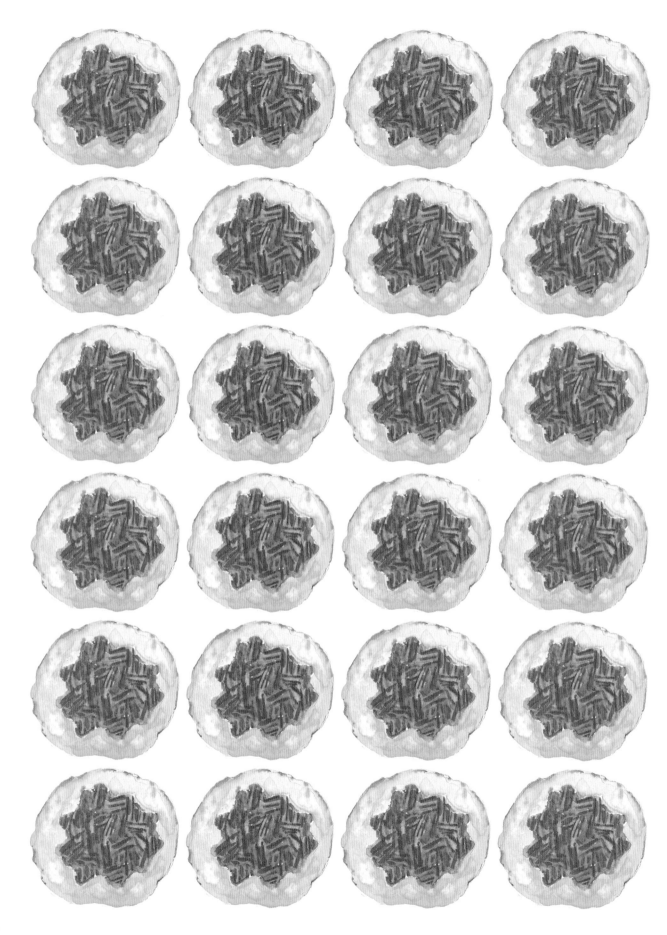

Rhubarb galette

For 6

To make the pie crust, place the flour and sugar in the food processor and pulse for 10 seconds. Add cold butter and pulse for 10 seconds. Beat the egg with a fork in a measuring jug and add enough cream to make up a ⅓ of a cup. While running the machine add the egg/cream mixture, once combined add the lemon juice – it should form a ball. Stop at this point and remove from the processor. Flatten to a disc shape (don't knead) and refrigerate for at least an hour.

Preheat your oven to 220°C.

Once chilled, roll out your pastry into a large circle (a bit bigger than a dinner plate) and transfer to some parchment paper. Return to the fridge for 15 minutes.

In the meantime, toss the rhubarb with lemon and sugar. Remove the pie crust from the fridge and sprinkle the amaretti biscuit in the middle of the tart leaving a 5 cm border of pastry for folding over. Then lay the rhubarb on top of the crumb in a zigzag pattern. Fold over the edges. Brush the edge with the beaten egg and sprinkle over the remaining sugar. Bake for 40 minutes or until golden.

Pie crust

165 g all-purpose flour

20 g sugar

115 g cold butter, diced

1 egg

30 g thickened cream

2 tsp lemon juice

Filling

500 g rhubarb, sliced into 7 cm batons

Juice of ½ a lemon

150 g sugar (keep a heaped table spoon aside)

4 amaretti biscuits, crushed into crumbs

1 egg, beaten

1.

2.

3.

4.

5.

6.

7.

8.

Tomatoes

♈	**Sow** mid-spring to midsummer
◎	**Harvest** summer, autumn
⊙	**Growing time** 12–16 weeks
⬥⬥	**Space between plants** 90 cm
⛁	**Pots** yes
☼	**Aspect** full sun
⎬	**Soil pH** 5.5–7.5
✳	**Frost tolerant** no
♡	**Companions** basil, asparagus, carrots, chives, nasturtiums, parsnips, borage, marigolds
◌	**Dislikes** rosemary, dill, potatoes, kohlrabi, fennel, strawberries

Tomatoes

1. Mortgage Lifter
2. Black cherry
3. Oxheart
4. Green tiger
5. Beefsteak
6. Truss cherry
7. Yellow pear cherry
8. Black Russian

Varieties

Grow lots of varieties to find your favourite. And don't forget the cherry tomatoes as they are probably the most generous plant in the vegetable patch.

Sow

Start seeds in a greenhouse or windowsill, or anywhere that is sunny and away from the danger of frost. Sow seeds into prepared seedling trays with seed-raising mix and water. Keep watered and in a warm spot (a heat mat can be used). They should be moist and not waterlogged. Plant out into their final spot when they are a good size seedling or when frosts are over.

Alternatively, garden centres will be full of nice-sized seedlings from the beginning of spring. I mostly buy my tomatoes like this. They seem to be way more advanced than my attempts in the greenhouse; however, it is much more economical to sow your own seeds.

Choose a sunny position with the correct amount of space for the number of plants you want. It is important to prepare your tomato beds well in advance of planting out. Dig in lots of compost and manure and give it time to settle in. Check the soil pH and adjust. Dig a hole deeper than your pot as you should plant tomatoes with the stem around 3–4 cm below the soil, as this will encourage more root growth.

Nurture

Think about staking tomatoes as you plant them out. The one time I didn't stake my tomatoes, boy was it a mess! I could hardly find the fruit and most of it was rotting underneath a sea of matted vines. I seem to try a different method every year. My next attempt will be to diligently secure each branch onto a purpose-built hard mesh frame. Three stakes secured then looped together with twine is a good one. I've used hoop frames, single stakes and obelisks, but most topple over with the weight of the vine or sag at the bottom in a tangled mess. Whatever method you use, make it sturdy.

→

Tomatoes require regular watering and should be watered at soil level and not on the leaves, or you risk getting fungal diseases. I highly recommend using the drip system on a timer. Another brilliant way of watering tomatoes is to use a soft drink bottle (see illustration). Water 2–3 times a week, but daily on hot days.

I mulch tomatoes with torn up cardboard placed around each plant and covered with straw. I find the cardboard helps to keep the fungal spores from the soil at bay. Feed your tomatoes with a high-potash fertiliser regularly once the flowers start to appear. Liquid feed fortnightly.

There are small shoots (laterals) in the elbows of tomato branches that are best pinched out. The easiest way to remove them is to pinch them with your fingernails. This encourages more fruit and fewer branches. Keep tying the plant to the trellis as it grows.

Harvest

Tomatoes are best ripened on the vine and picked regularly. *Never* store them in the fridge. The flavour is completely lost, if they are refrigerated. In autumn when the weather is starting to cool and ripening is slow, I usually sit my half-ripe tomatoes on the windowsill to ripen. When your tomato vine gives way to the frosts, harvest all the remaining green fruit and make chutney.

Tomato seeds can be collected by scooping the flesh into a sieve and rinsing under the tap before spreading them on paper towel to dry. Dry seeds can be left on the paper and stored in a jar in the pantry, for planting again next season.

How to grow tomatoes

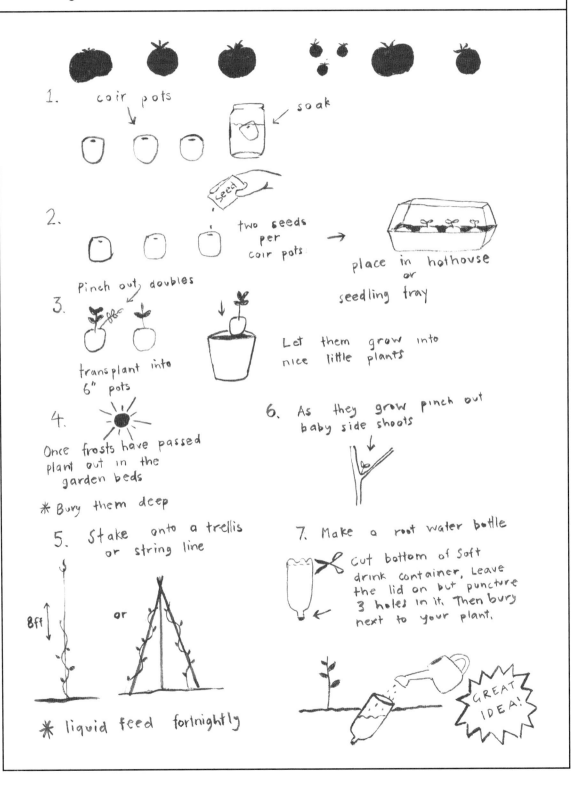

1. coir pots   soak

2. two seeds per coir pots → place in hothouse or seedling tray

Seed

3. Pinch out, doubles

transplant into 6" pots

Let them grow into nice little plants

4. Once frosts have passed plant out in the garden beds

* Bury them deep

5. Stake onto a trellis or string line

8ft   or

* liquid feed fortnightly

6. As they grow pinch out baby side shoots

7. Make a root water bottle

Cut bottom of soft drink container. Leave the lid on but puncture 3 holes in it. Then bury next to your plant.

GREAT IDEA!

Upside-down tomato and basil pie

For 6

from Belinda Jeffery's *Mix & Bake*

This is more like an upside-down cake than a pie. It is great for picnics.

....

Preheat the oven to 200°C. Grease a 26 cm diameter x 6 cm deep round ovenproof pie dish and line the base with greased baking paper. Set it aside.

Pour the tinned tomatoes into a sieve over a bowl and leave them to drain. Give them a stir occasionally to make sure as much juice as possible is removed.

Meanwhile, whiz the flour, salt and mustard powder together in a food processor. Add the cheeses and whiz again to just mix them in. Scatter the butter chunks over the top and process until the mixture resembles coarse breadcrumbs. Tip the mixture into a bowl.

In another bowl, whisk together the eggs, milk and Tabasco sauce. Make a well in the cheese mixture and pour in the egg mixture, then stir everything together to make a fairly stiff batter.

Lay the sliced tomatoes in overlapping circles in the base of the oven dish so the bottom is completely covered. Now spoon the drained tomatoes over the top and spread them out evenly (be a bit gentle doing this so you don't disturb the pattern of the sliced tomatoes). Sprinkle with the shredded basil. Dollop spoonfuls of the batter over the basil and tomatoes, then, with lightly floured hands, pat it out with your fingers to spread it evenly. Don't worry if there are a few little gaps; they fill out as the pie cooks.

Bake the pie for 30–35 minutes until the topping has risen and is golden. (The time will vary a bit depending on how thick your dish is.) Test it by inserting a thin skewer into the topping; if it comes out clean, the pie is ready. Remove the pie from the oven and leave it to settle in the dish for five minutes. Then sit a serving platter on top and carefully invert the pie onto it. Remove the pie dish and baking paper, then mop up any juices that seep out onto the plate.

Now just scatter some little basil leaves on top and drizzle with olive oil and it's ready to eat.

2 x 400 g tins chopped tomatoes

225 g self-raising flour

1 tsp salt

1 tsp dry mustard powder

100 g parmesan cheese, grated

50 g cheddar cheese, finely grated

125 g cold unsalted butter, cut into chunks

2 eggs

80 ml (⅓ cup) milk

A couple of shakes of Tabasco sauce

6 ripe tomatoes, thinly sliced (Roma tomatoes are ideal)

⅓ cup finely shredded basil leaves

Tiny basil leaves, to garnish

Olive oil, to drizzle

Varieties
Blackjack – dark green fruit, prolific
Golden – yellow fruit, prolific
Lebanese – light green, perfect for stuffing
Fordhook – green, lightly speckled

Zucchini

⚘	**Sow** mid-spring to midsummer
◎	**Harvest** summer, autumn
◔	**Growing time** 14 weeks
❦	**Space between plants** 1 m
⊽	**Pots** yes
☼	**Aspect** full sun
⏚	**Soil pH** 5.5–7.5
❋	**Frost tolerant** no
♡	**Companions** beans, corn, peas, radishes
◎	**Dislikes** potatoes

Sow

Start seeds in a greenhouse or on a windowsill, or anywhere that is sunny and away from the danger of frost. Zucchinis are easy to germinate. Sow seeds into prepared seedling trays with seed-raising mix and water. Keep watered and in a warm spot (a heat mat can be used). They should be moist, not waterlogged. Plant out into their final spot when they are a good-size seedling or when the risk of frost has passed. Give these seedlings lots of room to grow; the plant is easily 1 metre across. If growing from seedlings, divide the seedlings carefully from their punnet and plant directly into their position. Choose a sunny spot and prepare your soil well before planting. A good layer of compost, manure and mulch to top it. Seeds can be planted in situ after frosts.

Nurture

You can create a little polytunnel with clear plastic sheeting and hoops to get seedlings started. Or use soft drink bottles with their bottoms cut off as greenhouse cloches. Zucchinis are very prolific plants, so for the average family 2–3 plants are more than enough. They are also very large plants, so if space is a problem even one will yield more than enough zucchinis. Water zucchinis in the morning and water low to avoid watering the leaves. Zucchinis are susceptible to a white mould, which is a fungus that can spread to other plants. Keep plants well watered during the hottest months. They respond well to watering with an upturned soft drink bottle buried beside the plant. Zucchinis have male and female flowers and pollination is vital for the formation of fruit. Mostly the bees and insects will do that for you, but if fruit isn't forming you can pick a male flower (the ones with no swollen base) and play God by connecting the anthers with the female stigmas of the flowers on the plant. Liquid feed your plants fortnightly.

Harvest

Once they get going it is all on! Harvesting needs to happen almost daily as they go from an easy pick to needing a forklift within a day. The ideal size to pick is 10–15 cm for the best flavour. I like to leave the Lebanese zucchinis until they are approximately 20 cm so that I can stuff them with veal mince, tomato and rice, then cook them in passata in the oven. The flowers can also be harvested for stuffing with soft goat's cheese, herbs and pine nuts, then battered and deep fried.

Zucchini and feta fritters

For 6

The zucchini in this recipe can be swapped with many different vegetables and when it's late in the day and you haven't even thought about what you are going to dish up for dinner this recipe delivers big time. Variations are carrot, corn, potato, celeriac, kohlrabi, pea, pumpkin, cauliflower, onion. Basil, tarragon, parsley, thyme, rosemary and chives can also be called on for a variation of flavour.

Grate the zucchini and put them in a colander in the sink. Sprinkle with salt and set aside for 5–10 minutes.

In a medium bowl, beat the egg and combine with the flour, parmesan, chilli, lemon rind and mint.

Squeeze out the zucchini and add it to the batter. Crumble the feta into the mixture. If you would like a looser batter, just add a bit of milk.

Heat a shallow layer of oil in a heavy-based frying pan and drop spoonfuls of batter into the hot oil, being careful not to overcrowd the pan. Don't make the fritters too big: four to a pan is good. Flip when well cooked on one side. Keep cooked fritters warm by putting them on a baking tray in the oven (200°C) while you are cooking the rest of the batter. This ensures that the fritters are cooked through, as they can be hard to judge in the pan.

Serve with rocket leaves dressed with the lemon juice, or a poached egg.

3 large zucchini

1 tbsp salt

1 egg

25 g plain flour

20 g parmesan cheese, grated

1 small red chilli, deseeded and finely chopped

1 lemon, rind finely grated, juiced

1 handful of mint, leaves picked, chopped

100 g feta cheese

Milk, to loosen batter (optional)

Oil, to shallow fry

Rocket leaves or poached eggs, to serve (optional)

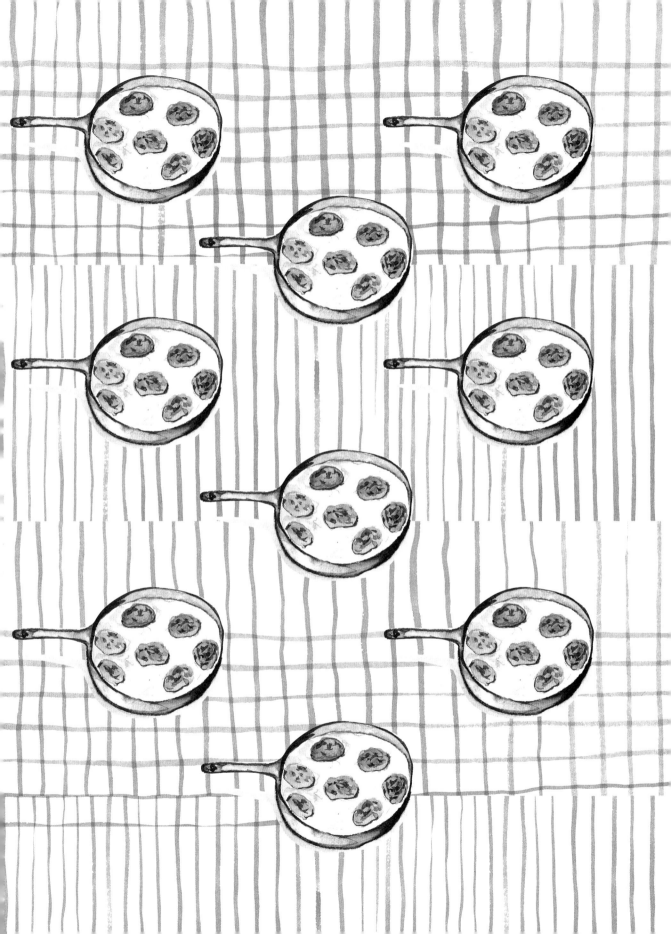

Chapter 02

Summertime planting

Your vegetable garden should be well underway by the beginning of summer. By the middle of the season your basket should be brimming with vegetables such as tomatoes, cucumbers, capsicums, beans, chillies, eggplants and zucchinis. If you are growing fruit, you should be eating plums, apricots, berries, melons, nectarines, pears, apples and more. Summer is the time to set up a table under a tree with a nice cloth and enjoy the outdoors while eating simple and fresh ingredients straight from your own garden. At this time of year the vegetables usually determine the menu. I am a believer in not overcomplicating things, so it might mean just adding a good glug of beautiful extra virgin olive oil, flaky salt and a squeeze of lemon; homegrown vegetables usually taste better, mostly because of their freshness – they haven't been carted from one end of the country to another in a refrigerated truck. Remember to stay vigilant about keeping water up to your vegetables. Check your soil for dryness by pushing your finger into the garden beds. It should feel moist from your second knuckle down. It's also a time to keep birdbaths full and add a few extra bowls of water for wildlife and pets. Hot days are good for staying inside in the cool and pickling, dehydrating and preserving all your excess fruit and vegetables. By doing this you will take a little bit of the summer joy through into the winter months.

Varieties
Red Rubine aka *Ruby* – plum colour
Trafalgar – reliable, large sprouts
Oliver – high yield
Red Ribs – reddish
Drumtight – robust, adaptable

Brussels sprouts

♈ **Sow** summer

◎ **Harvest** autumn, winter

◷ **Growing time** 30–36 weeks

✔✔ **Space between plants** 60 cm

▽ **Pots** possible

☼ **Aspect** full sun

⬇ **Soil pH** 6.8–7.5

✳ **Frost tolerant** yes

♡ **Companions** brassicas, turnips, parsnips, beetroot, onions, marigolds, carrots, celery, silverbeet, cucumbers, garlic, lettuce, potatoes, basil, chives, artichokes, rhubarb, borage

◎ **Dislikes** tomatoes, strawberries, capsicums, eggplant

Sow

Fill seedling trays with seed-raising mix and water in. Push seeds into the depth of 1–2 cm at 5 cm apart and water them lightly. Once they have emerged, remove the weaker seedlings and plant out the stronger ones when they are 6–8 cm tall.

The planting time with Brussels sprouts is important. They have a very long growing time, usually 5 months. Start them off in summer for a winter harvest. Use lots of compost and rotted manure to prepare the soil.

Nurture

Cover plants with a fine net to keep away the dreaded cabbage moths, and also watch for aphids. You can dust with derris powder (a natural insecticide available from garden centres) if need be. The plants will need staking to a 1 metre wooden stake as they grow. When the bottom sprouts are quite small, start pulling off the lower leaves with a sideways pull, allowing the sprouts to develop more easily.

Harvest

Harvest the sprouts as they get to size and are firm. Start your harvest from the bottom where the sprouts will be more mature. The best way to harvest is by twisting them off. The leaves at the top are good to use in salads and to sauté.

Pickled Brussels sprouts

Makes 2 small preserving jars

In a large saucepan of boiling salted water, cook Brussels sprouts for about 3–5 minutes until tender. Drain and rinse under cold water. Pack into sterilised preserving jars (see p. 190) layered with dill and garlic. Place a bay leaf inside each jar.

Return the saucepan to medium heat and put in 250 ml (1 cup) of water with the remaining ingredients. Bring to a boil and simmer until salt and sugar has dissolved.

Carefully pour the hot brine into the sterilised jars until full. Set aside to cool to room temperature. Seal jars and refrigerate for at least 3 hours before serving. Store in the fridge for up to 3 months.

500 g Brussels sprouts, trimmed and halved
1 small handful of fresh dill sprigs
1 small garlic clove, thinly sliced
250 ml (1 cup) water
250 ml (1 cup) white vinegar
1 tsp black peppercorns
1 tbsp yellow mustard seeds
2 bay leaves
½ tsp crushed chilli flakes
2 tsp kosher salt or any salt without iodine
½ cup granulated sugar

Capsicums

♈	**Sow** late spring, summer
◎	**Harvest** summer, autumn
◷	**Growing time** 20–26 weeks
♈♈	**Space between plants** 40 cm
⛁	**Pots** yes
☼	**Aspect** full sun
⚖	**Soil pH** 6.8–7.5
✳	**Frost tolerant** no
♡	**Companions** carrots, parsnips, tomatoes, eggplant, chillies
◠	**Dislikes** fennel, potatoes, bok choy, broccoli, Brussels sprouts, cauliflower, kale, kohlrabi, rocket, radishes

Sow

Start seeds off undercover at the end of winter or early spring (see p. 165). Plant out when they are 15 cm tall and the weather is warm with no threat of frosts. Capsicums love heat so find a sunny spot. Seedlings should be planted out at 30–40 cm spacing in rows. They need staking to the height of 60 cm.

Nurture

Keep plants well watered and feed regularly with a high-potash liquid fertiliser. This is particularly important when the fruit appears. Often the plant will start off with one large fruit which should be picked while green and this will encourage subsequent fruit growth.

Harvest

Fruit will start off green and move through to a deep red (or other colour, if you've planted one of the coloured varieties) if left on the plant. It can be harvested at any point. When harvesting fruit leave a small amount of stem on the fruit as this will help its storage length.

Stuffed capsicums

For 6

Preheat the oven to 220°C. Cut the tops off the capsicum to scoop out and discard the seeds and membrane.

In a large bowl, mix together the rice, mince, onion, tomato, pine nuts, currants and spices, and spoon into the capsicums. Replace the lids. Place in a high-sided baking dish (preferably one that just fits the capsicums). Pour the stock around the capsicums and cover with aluminium foil.

Bake for 50 minutes in total. Spoon stock over the capsicums a few times throughout the cooking time. After 20 minutes, remove the foil and cook for another 30 minutes.

Meanwhile, mix the yoghurt, dill, garlic and lemon juice together in a small bowl.

Serve stuffed capsicums slightly warm or at room temperature with the yoghurt mixture on the side.

6 capsicums – choose square-shaped fruit that sits upright on its base
150 g uncooked rice
150 g lamb or pork mince
1 large onion, finely chopped
2 large tomatoes, finely chopped
50 g pine nuts, toasted
50 g currants
1 tsp ground allspice
1 tsp ground cinnamon
400 ml chicken stock
300 g Greek yoghurt
10 g dill
1 garlic clove, crushed or finely chopped
1 tbsp lemon juice

STUFFED

Varieties
California Wonder (aka *Giant Bell*) – large fruit, sweet
Orange Bell, *Orange Sun* – good yields, orange colour
Purple Beauty – dark purple, looks good in salads

Carrots

♈	**Sow** spring, summer (all year in some areas)
◎	**Harvest** spring, autumn
◷	**Growing time** 12–20 weeks
♥♥	**Space between plants** 5 cm
▽	**Pots** yes (large)
☼	**Aspect** full sun
⬇	**Soil pH** 5.8–7.0
❄	**Frost tolerant** yes
♡	**Companions** beans, peas, capsicums, chillies, Brussels sprouts, kale, kohlrabi, chives, lettuce, leeks, sage, marigolds
◎	**Dislikes** dill, parsnips, celery, potatoes

Varieties

Baby – sweet, finger length
Manchester Table – popular, deep orange
Purple Dragon – purple with orange centre
Topweight – popular
Egmont Gold – reliable

Sow

In warmer areas carrots can be grown all year round. In cooler areas the growth time is about 6–8 weeks from midwinter until the beginning of autumn.

Sow seeds directly into well-prepared soil with manure or all-round fertiliser added. They don't like being transplanted. Gardeners with clay soil will need to create a friable and loose soil to be able to grow any root vegetables: sand can be added to the compost. Sow seeds in rows or just en masse and thin out if overcrowded.

Nurture

Liquid feed carrots fortnightly. Plant with marigolds to distract carrot flies. Carrots like regular watering but are fairly hardy.

Harvest

Pull carrots when needed, usually 12 weeks after sowing. Carrots that remain in the ground after winter will go to seed in spring. The flowers are quite beautiful, and are sometimes known as Queen Anne's Lace. Leave until dried out and collect seeds in a brown paper bag.

Spiced carrot jam

Makes 4 medium preserving jars

Put all ingredients in a non-reactive saucepan and boil for around 10–15 minutes until translucent. Use the jam testing method on p. 190 to check if your jam is ready. Once ready, pour into warmed sterilised jars (see p. 190) and set aside to cool. Store in the fridge for up to 6 weeks. Great served with cheese.

700 g carrots, grated
600 g sugar
125 ml (½ cup) lemon juice
6 cardamom pods, bruised
1 tbsp dried chilli flakes

Cauliflower

Sow late summer, autumn

Harvest winter, spring

Growing time 20–26 weeks

Space between plants 45 cm

Pots possible

Aspect full sun

Soil pH 6.8–7.5

Frost tolerant yes

Companions everything except those listed below

Dislikes tomatoes, strawberries, capsicums, eggplant

Varieties

Snowball – sow in spring for autumn harvest
Violet Queen – purple, but turns green when cooked
All the Year Round – as the name states
Mini – small heads

Sow

Sow seeds into punnets or seed trays (see p. 165) or sow directly into the garden. Prepare soil with compost and rotted manure and top with mulch (see p. 162). The seeds can be scattered in a row and thinned out if there are excess plants. Sow 2 cm deep. Plants need to be 45 cm apart. Avoid planting where other brassica crops have been to reduce the chance of soil diseases. (See crop rotation p. 184.)

Nurture

Watch for slugs and snails. They can take out all your seedlings at once at this early stage. Make a death trap of beer in a cup or tin (see p. 186). Netting is a good idea as the cabbage moth is also a pest. Aphids can be controlled with natural sprays (see p. 187). Fertilise regularly with a liquid fertiliser. Always make sure your plants are well watered. When the cauliflower forms a head, pull up the surrounding leaves and clip them together at the top to completely cover the white heads. This protects the curds (florets) from going yellow from either frost or sunburn.

Harvest

When the cauliflower heads reach the desired size, cut them from the base of the plant. Store in the fridge and use the younger leaves in stews or soups.

Risotto al cavolfiore

For 4

Heat the stock in a large saucepan and keep it hot. Break up the cauliflower into small pieces and add to the stock.

Heat the olive oil in a large, deep frying pan on medium heat and fry the onion, celery and garlic very gently until soft. Add the rice and stir for a few minutes to coat the rice in oil. When it looks translucent, add the wine and keep stirring. When the rice has absorbed the wine, ladle in the stock and cauliflower, one spoonful at a time, stirring constantly and waiting each time for the rice to take up the stock.

When you notice that the rice grains are swollen, test to see if there is just a small amount of resistance in the middle (al dente). Then add the parmesan and butter. Swirl until creamy and remove from the heat. Taste and season with salt and pepper. Cover with a clean tea towel and let it rest for a few minutes.

Fry the breadcrumbs in oil. Serve risotto topped with the crumbs, parsley and grated parmesan cheese.

1 litre (4 cups) chicken or vegetable stock
1 small cauliflower
2 tbsp olive oil, plus extra for frying
1 brown onion, finely chopped (optional)
1 celery stalk, finely chopped
2 garlic cloves, chopped
400 g risotto rice
500 ml (2 cups) dry white wine
115 g parmesan cheese, grated
50 g butter
1½ cups breadcrumbs made from a stale loaf
Finely chopped parsley and grated parmesan cheese, to serve
Salt and pepper

Chillies

♈	**Sow** late spring, summer
◎	**Harvest** summer, autumn
◷	**Growing time** 20–26 weeks
⚏	**Space between plants** 40 cm
⛁	**Pots** yes
☼	**Aspect** full sun
⚖	**Soil pH** 6.8–7.5
✳	**Frost tolerant** no
♡	**Companions** carrots, parsnips, tomatoes, eggplant, capsicums
⌒	**Dislikes** fennel, potatoes

Chillies

1. Thai
2. Habanero
3. Long green
4. Long red
5. Cherry pepper
6. Pepperoncini
7. Jalapeño
8. Birdseye
9. Scotch bonnet
10. Poblano

Sow

Start seedlings off undercover at the end of winter/early spring (see p. 165) or direct sow in late spring for a summer crop. Plant out when they are 15 cm tall and the weather is warm and there is no threat of frosts. Chillies love heat so find a sunny spot. Seedlings should be planted out at 30–40 cm spacing in rows.

Nurture

Keep plants well watered and feed regularly with a high-potash liquid fertiliser. This is particularly important when the fruit appears. Some plants might need staking. Plants in pots need extra watering as they tend to dry out more quickly.

Harvest

Chillies can be harvested when they get to the desired size. Immature green chillies will have a milder taste and the mature red ones will have a hotter taste. They can be picked or snipped off. When frosts come, you can pull the whole plant and hang it upside down in the greenhouse to dry. When dried you can crush the chillies to make chilli flakes and store in a jar.

Chilli jam

Makes 4 medium preserving jars

Chop the chillies finely by hand or use a food processor. Add all the ingredients to a heavy base pan and boil until it becomes jammy and sticky, this usually takes 20 minutes or so. Test your jam using the method on p. 190. If your jam is ready, pour into sterilised jars (p. 190) and seal. Store in the fridge for 3–4 months.

150 g fresh red chillies, stalks removed
225 ml apple cider vinegar
500 g sugar

CHILLI JAM

1.

2.

3.

4.

5.

6.

7.

Pumpkin

Sow spring, summer

Harvest summer, autumn

Growing time 18–22 weeks

Space between plants 1 m

Pots yes

Aspect full sun, part shade

Soil pH 6.8–7.5

Frost tolerant no

Companions beans, corn, melons, zucchini

Dislikes potatoes

Sow
Pumpkins have a very long growing period. Getting them started undercover gives them a head start. Prepare your seed pots (see p. 165). Sow seeds 2 cm deep into 10 cm pots in late winter or early spring. Once frosts have passed, plant out to an area that will allow them to sprawl.

To sow directly into the ground in mid-spring, sow 3 cm deep, 1 m apart into well-cultivated soil (see p. 158).

Nurture
Pumpkins are hungry plants and will need regular liquid feeds. The flowers might need help pollinating if the bees aren't doing their job. Brush the anther from the male flower over the stigma in the female flower. Keep well watered through the hotter months.

Harvest
During autumn the cold will set in and the pumpkins will be ready for harvest. Sometimes they are ready before this and will have a hollow sound when you knock on their skin. Cut the stems short and leave the pumpkins in a sunny spot for at least a week to dry off. They can then be stored for months in a cool, dry, dark room or store.

Pumpkins

1. Turk's Turban
2. Butternut
3. Queensland blue
4. Kabocha
5. Cinderella (Rouge Vif d'Etampes)
6. Sweet Dumpling
7. Red Kuri (potimarron)

Pumpkin and eschalot tarte Tatin

For 6

Preheat the oven to 220°C.

Place the eschalots and pumpkin on a baking tray and drizzle over olive oil. Bake for 20 minutes or until the pumpkin is soft but not coloured.

Meanwhile in a 24 cm fry pan (one that is able to be put in the oven) melt the brown sugar and butter until bubbling, then add thyme. Once finished in the oven, dot the pumpkin and eschalots in a pretty mosaic tiled pattern around the pan. They should be snug. Fry for 10 minutes (undisturbed) until the vegetables start to caramelise. Remove from heat.

Place the pastry on top of vegetables and tuck in the excess pastry all around the edges using a spoon. If you are using sheet pastry use a double layer.

Place in the oven for 20 minutes or until the puff pastry is puffed and golden brown. To turn out the tart, place a plate (that is larger than your pan) upside down on the top of the pan, place one hand on the plate and a gloved hand on the pan handle and quickly flip ... do it with confidence and all will be fine!

Half a butternut pumpkin, peeled and chopped into pieces the size of a matchbox

8 small eschalots, peeled

2 tbsp extra virgin olive oil

4 tbsp brown sugar

50 g butter

3 tbsp red wine vinegar

4 sprigs of thyme, leaves picked

350 g puff pastry (rolled to 26cm round) or 2 sheets of bought pastry

*The best quality pastry will result in a more spectacular tart. Some bakeries will sell blocks of puff pastry which is ideal.

Chapter 03

Autumn planting

Arguably, autumn is one of the best seasons in the garden. The garden tends to kick back and do its own thing at this time of year. Any struggle against the heat dissipates and the sun is gentle and inviting. The vegetable patch is often at its wild and woolliest. Tomatoes are like a jungle and become too heavy for their frames. Zucchinis that escape being picked end up giant in size. Pumpkin tendrils march across the garden and up fences. Preserving is a full-time job at this time of year. Quinces, raspberries, figs, fennel, apples, zucchinis, eggplants, chillies and tomatoes are all ready to be bottled for the coming months. Autumn is also the time to sow winter vegetables. Kale, cabbage, broccoli, broad beans, garlic: get them in before the cold sets in. Prepare your beds and protect your vegetables with a good layer of mulch ... just like tucking them into bed!

Beetroot

🌱 **Sow** autumn, winter, spring

◎ **Harvest** spring, early summer

🕐 **Growing time** 10–16 weeks

🌱 **Space between plants** 10 cm

🪴 **Pots** yes (large)

☀ **Aspect** full sun

⚓ **Soil pH** 5.8–7.0

❄ **Frost tolerant** yes

♡ **Companions** brassicas, kohlrabi, onions, silverbeet, cabbage

⊘ **Dislikes** beans, tomatoes

Varieties

Derwent Globe – popular
Burpee's Golden – golden
Baby beetroot, such as *Babybeat* – ready in 6 weeks

Sow

I recommend direct planting. Prepare the soil (see p. 158). Create a line about 2 cm deep and sprinkle in seeds, aiming for about 5 cm apart. You will need to thin these out when they are bigger to create 10 cm spaces between plants. Water in gently. It's a good idea to do succession planting, where you stagger sowing and planting your seeds, to keep a long supply happening.

Nurture

Beetroot responds well to fortnightly liquid feeds and produces a nice-tasting crop with a regular and consistent supply of water.

Harvest

Harvest beetroot when it's the correct size – golf ball for small varieties and tennis ball for larger varieties. Beets will grow on top of the soil, so don't attempt to cover them.

Beet tart with thyme and honey

For 6

Peel and slice 400 g of beetroot 1 cm thick and spread them on a baking tray or dish. Drizzle with olive oil and honey and add a splash of balsamic vinegar. Roast in a hot oven (200°C) for 30 minutes. Slice a red onion, scatter it over the beetroot and cook for a further 20 minutes.

Roll out some puff pastry (or use frozen) and line a shallow tart dish. Add the beets and onion plus about 200 g of feta and sprinkle with fresh thyme leaves. Bake for 20–30 minutes. Nice with a lemony, zesty pile of rocket.

– SALAD

– DEHYDRATE

PICKLE –

PICKLE

– BOIL

– ROAST

– DEHYDRATE

Broad beans

♈	**Sow** autumn, winter
◎	**Harvest** spring, early summer
☉	**Growing time** 12–24 weeks
❧❧	**Space between plants** 30 cm
☷	**Pots** yes (large)
☀	**Aspect** full sun
⎍	**Soil pH** 5.8–7.0
✳	**Frost tolerant** yes
♡	**Companions** carrots, marigolds, eggplant, potatoes
⌒	**Dislikes** beetroot, onions, garlic, sunflowers

Varieties

Aquadulce – early fruiter, good flavour

Evergreen or *Coles Early Dwarf* – heavy croppers, medium sized pods

Crimson Flowered – beautiful crimson flower

Sow

Seedlings can be raised undercover, but really they are better planted directly in their spot; however, if you are waiting for another crop to finish, you can get a head start by sowing into small pots.

Broad beans have a long taproot so toilet roll cores make good growing tubes for broad beans. Put one in each pot with a little seed-raising mix. Plant out when the seedling is strong.

Sow 5 cm deep into well-watered and prepared soil (see p. 158). Plant 30 cm apart in rows that form a block, that way they kind of support each other. Too much space around them can cause them to topple. I tend to create a 'fence' around them with wooden stakes and twine, that holds them all together in a block. Water well when planting out seeds, then don't water again until seedlings appear after 10 days or so.

Nurture

Extra fertiliser is usually unnecessary with broad beans. You can liquid feed if you feel they need a push along, but don't overdo it.

Harvest

Pick pods when they are swollen with beans. They will start to ripen quite quickly once they are ready. Pick every couple of days to keep up. If left too long they can become bitter and will need double podding as the inner skin of the bean becomes tough.

Bruschetta with broad beans

For 4

Anything with toast as a vehicle is a winner in my eyes but this one is next level. By the way, the correct way to pronounce bruschetta is with a 'K' sound not a 'SH' sound (glad I've got that off my chest)! Blanch 2 cups of podded broad beans in boiling water, then drain and refresh in cold water. Remove skins. Use a fork to crush the beans on a chopping board. Gather them into a bowl and drizzle with *good* extra virgin olive oil. Add some finely chopped mint, a pinch of salt flakes and a squeeze of lemon juice, to taste. Grill 4 pieces of sourdough bread. Rub with the cut side of a garlic clove. Top with the bean mixture and shave thin slivers of parmesan on top. You can also sprinkle on a pinch of chilli flakes if you feel inclined. Or try the bean mixture with feta and an egg as a breakfast option.

Varieties

Shogun – good in summer and winter
Purple Sprouting – purple, multi-stems
Romanesco – likes cool weather, eccentric shape

Broccoli

♈	**Sow** all year
◎	**Harvest** all year
☉	**Growing time** 12–16 weeks
✿✿	**Space between plants** 35 cm
☐	**Pots** possible
☼	**Aspect** full sun
⚓	**Soil pH** 5.8–7.0
✳	**Frost tolerant** yes
♡	**Companions** beetroot, onions, marigolds, carrots, celery, silverbeet, cucumbers, garlic, lettuce, potatoes, basil, chives, artichokes, rhubarb, borage
◎	**Dislikes** tomatoes, strawberries, capsicums, eggplant

Sow

Sow seeds into seedling trays with seed-raising mix or into coir pods. Plant two seeds together and the weaker plants can be thinned out. Bury 1 cm deep and keep well watered. Plant out when the seedling is robust and has 3 or 4 leaves. Direct planting can be done in rows 30 cm apart in full sun. Sow a sparse sprinkling of seeds to a depth of 2 cm. They can be thinned out later if necessary.

Store-bought punnets can be planted out at 45 cm apart.

Nurture

You will more than likely need to net your plants as cabbage moths will descend on them rather enthusiastically. The net needs to be a fine weave. You can use derris powder if need be. A fertiliser high in nitrogen can be added once the flower heads have formed (not before, as this will encourage the side shoots). Rotate your broccoli crop with a different crop in the next planting to reduce the risk of further infestation of pests.

Harvest

Harvesting is usually 8–10 weeks from planting out. Cut the main head first, leaving the bulk of the plant. Subsequent harvesting can be from the outer shoots. The leaves of the plant can also be eaten. Store in the fridge.

Sicilian orecchiette with broccoli

For 4

Bring two large saucepans of well-salted water to the boil. Add the orecchiette to one and the broccoli to the other, stir and cook for 8–9 minutes or until the pasta is al dente and the broccoli has just gone soft. Heat the oil in a large frying pan over medium heat. Add the anchovies and break them up into the oil, then add garlic, chilli and a little of the pasta cooking water. Chop the soft broccoli, add to the pan and fry until it breaks down. When the pasta is al dente, use a large slotted spoon to transfer the pasta into the pan with the anchovy/broccoli mixture, along with some more pasta cooking water. Toss together for 1 minute or until well combined, then serve topped with the fried breadcrumbs and grated parmesan cheese.

400 g orecchiette pasta

300 g broccoli florets, including leaves and finely sliced stems if you like

50 ml extra virgin olive oil

6 anchovies

2 garlic cloves, finely chopped

1 small chilli, finely chopped

100 g fresh breadcrumbs, fried in butter or olive oil

Grated parmesan cheese, to serve

Cabbage

♈	**Sow** all year
◎	**Harvest** all year
◔	**Growing time** 18–24 weeks
♈♈	**Space between plants** 40 cm
☗	**Pots** possible
☀	**Aspect** full sun
⚓	**Soil pH** 6.8–7.5
❋	**Frost tolerant** yes
♡	**Companions** everything except those listed below
☹	**Dislikes** tomatoes, strawberries, capsicums, eggplant

Varieties
Savoy – large blistered leaves
Red – glossy red leaves
Sugarloaf – sweet

Sow
Sow undercover. Prepare seedling trays (see p. 165). Plant seeds 2 cm deep and water gently. Once they are a few centimetres high you can move them to coir pots and raise till they are 15 cm, then plant them out. Young plants are vulnerable to slugs and snails so be careful to protect them. Plastic domes can be made from cut-down soft drink bottles.

Store-bought seedlings are probably the easiest way to start your cabbage patch, and can be planted out at any time of year.

You can direct sow into the soil at 2 cm deep. Prepare the soil (see p. 158). Plant more than you need so you can pull out the weaker seedlings once they have begun to grow. You need to allow 40 cm between each plant. The cabbages will need to be netted to protect them from cabbage moths, especially in the summer months. The net needs to be fine and taut.

Nurture
A fertiliser high in nitrogen is good for healthy cabbages. Chicken manure is particularly good. Keep your plants well watered throughout the summer months. Water the soil rather than the leaves to prevent rot.

Harvest
The cabbages are ready to harvest when they reach the desired size. They can be sliced from the base or pulled.

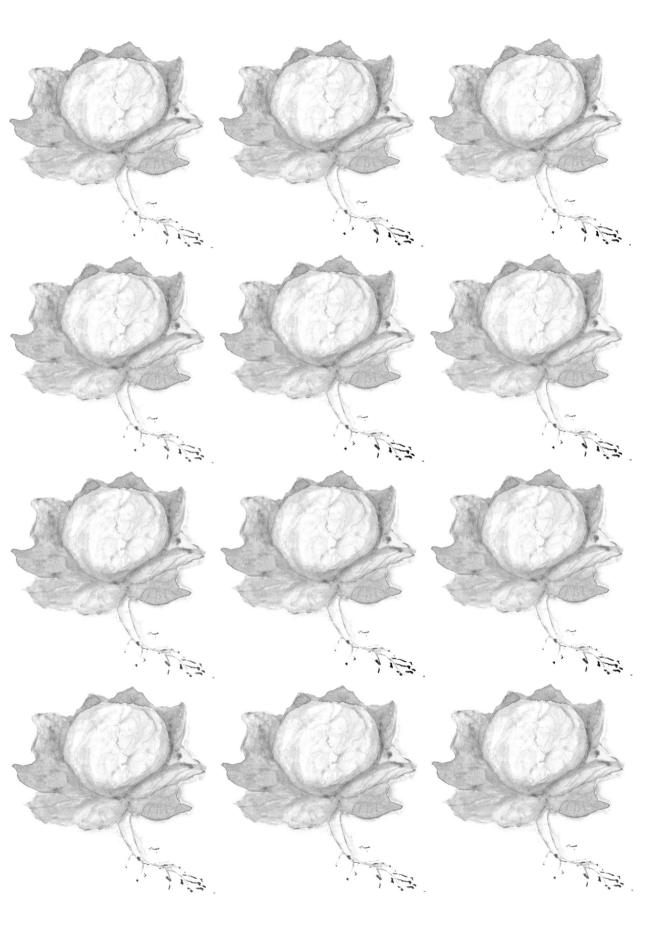

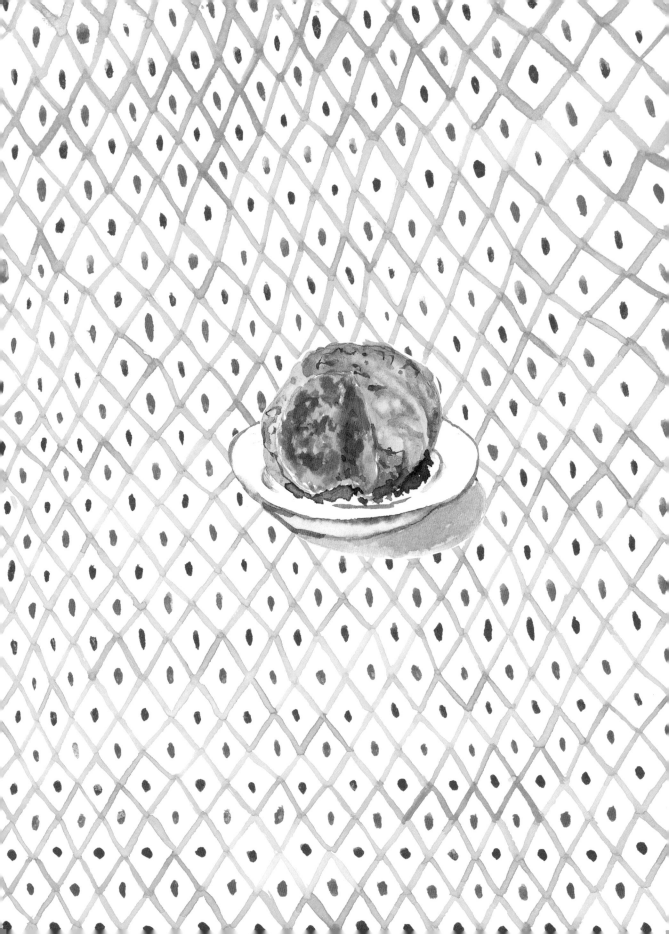

Lou fassum (stuffed cabbage)

For 4

Bring a large saucepan of water to the boil. Meanwhile, using a sharp, short-bladed knife, core the cabbage. Remove at least 20 intact outer leaves. Thinly slice 2 cups of the remaining raw cabbage and set aside.

Boil the leaves for 2 minutes and refresh in iced water. Work in batches.

Put the rice into a small saucepan of boiling water and cook for 4 minutes. Drain and set aside.

Heat 100 ml of the olive oil in a large frying pan on medium-high heat. Add the garlic and onion and cook for 3 minutes until translucent. Add the mushrooms, ½ teaspoon salt and some pepper. Cook, stirring frequently, for 3 minutes or until softened. Add the thinly sliced cabbage and the chard and cook for about 5 minutes until wilted.

Transfer the vegetables to a baking sheet and spread into an even layer. Refrigerate for 10–15 minutes until completely cool.

In a large bowl, mix the pork, ham, prosciutto and bacon. Add the tomato, rice, sautéed vegetables, peas, cheese and lemon rind. Add the remaining olive oil, 2 teaspoons of salt and a generous amount of black pepper; mix well.

Line a large, round-bottomed bowl with a clean linen tea towel or 3 layers of cheesecloth (there should be significant overhang). Starting with the largest leaves, lay the blanched cabbage pieces on top of the towel, arranging them stem side down in a concave manner, overlapping the leaves significantly to create a sphere with sturdy layers. Transfer the filling to the cabbage-lined bowl, pressing down with your hands to compact. Tuck the leaves in as needed to fully enclose the filling and shape the lou fassum into a neat, firmly packed, liquid-tight sphere. Wrap the edges of the towel around the cabbage so they meet at the top centre. Using twine, tie the towel very tightly to make sure the lou fassum holds its shape.

In a large, deep saucepan, bring the prepared stock to a boil and lower the lou fassum into the pot. Simmer gently over low heat for 2 hours, adding water if necessary to keep the whole cabbage covered. Lift from stock. Serve cut into wedges, with mashed potatoes.

1 large Savoy cabbage

1¼ cups long-grain rice

160 ml olive oil

1 large garlic head, peeled and chopped (⅓ cup)

1 large onion, peeled and chopped (2½ cups)

150 g mushrooms, sliced

Salt and pepper

1 bunch Swiss chard, stems removed, leaves thinly sliced (3 cups)

1 kg pork mince

150 g cooked ham, julienned but not too fine (1 cup)

6 thin slices prosciutto, torn

10 slices unsmoked bacon or pancetta (½ cup, firmly packed)

4 large tomatoes, chopped

1½ cups fresh or frozen peas

1½ cups finely grated parmesan or pecorino cheese

Finely grated rind of ½ lemon

4 litres (16 cups) chicken stock, homemade or ready-made

Mashed potato, to serve

Garlic

♈	**Sow** autumn
◎	**Harvest** early summer
☉	**Growing time** 20–36 weeks
▼▼	**Space between plants** 15–18 cm
▽	**Pots** possible
☼	**Aspect** full sun
⎯⏚	**Soil pH** 6.8–7.5
❄	**Frost tolerant** yes
♡	**Companions** everything except those listed below
⌒	**Dislikes** beans, broad beans, peas

Varieties
New Zealand Purple – popular, easy to peel
Russian or *Elephant garlic* – large and less pungent
Italian White – long-lasting bulbs

Sow
Garlic is best planted out directly. Choose a sunny position and cultivate the soil (see p. 158).

You will need good strong planting bulbs to start your crop. These can be sourced from your local garden centre or from saved cloves from last year's crop. Separate the cloves and choose the largest ones to plant out. Press the individual cloves into the soil at 7–10 cm intervals. They should be buried to the depth of twice the length of the clove with the tip facing up. Water in well.

Nurture
The cloves need watering regularly in the beginning, but once they are established they are okay with watering once or twice a week.

Harvest
There is a long wait until garlic is ready for harvest. Usually, this is at the beginning of summer when the foliage has started to turn yellow and die down. Gently ease bulbs from the soil by using a garden fork.

To dry your garlic, choose a dry sunny spot and rest them flat on wire racks for at least two weeks. They are ready for hanging once the skins have dried and feel crisp. The garlic stems can be braided at this stage. Hang them upside down in a cool dry area to store.

Preserved garlic in oil

Peel several heads of garlic cloves. Put them into a saucepan and cover with apple cider vinegar and a couple of tablespoons of sugar. Boil for 2–3 minutes until just soft. Drain and keep vinegar for other uses. Put the garlic in sterilised jars (see p. 190). Add a bay leaf and some peppercorns. Pour in enough oil (use a light oil such as grapeseed oil) to cover and seal the jar. Preserved garlic can be stored in the fridge for several months.

Bagna cauda with crudités

For 4–8 as a dip

My sister, who is an amazing cook, introduced me to this dish 30 years ago. It's simple but very punchy.

....

Combine anchovies, oil and garlic in a small saucepan over medium heat until it all meshes together and the anchovies and garlic are soft. Whisk in the butter until dissolved. Add more butter if the taste is too pungent. Serve warm in a small bowl that has been preheated, surrounded with the vegetables for dipping.

15 anchovy fillets, chopped

125 ml (½ cup) extra virgin olive oil

5 garlic cloves, finely chopped

125 g unsalted butter, cut into cubes

Raw vegetables, such as celery, carrots, broccoli, cut into bite size crudités, to serve

Kohlrabi

🌱 **Sow** autumn, winter

◎ **Harvest** spring, summer

🕐 **Growing time** 6–12 weeks

Space between plants 25 cm

Pots yes (large)

☀ **Aspect** full sun

Soil pH 5.8–7.0

❄ **Frost tolerant** yes

♡ **Companions** beetroot, onions, marigolds, carrots, celery, silverbeet, cucumbers, garlic, lettuce, potatoes, basil, chives, artichokes, rhubarb, borage

⊙ **Dislikes** tomatoes, strawberries, capsicums, eggplant

Varieties

Emerald – lime green
Early Purple Vienna – purple
Sweet Vienna – white

Sow

Sow directly into soil that has been well prepared with manure or all-round fertiliser. Create rows 40 cm apart and place seeds 25 cm apart. Seedlings should appear 10 days later and must be protected from slugs and snails. Seeds can be raised undercover and transplanted once the seedling is strong.

Nurture

Kohlrabi is susceptible to cabbage moths, so netting is a good idea. They are best grown quickly and liquid feeding will help with that. The bulb sits on top of the soil and is one of the craziest looking vegetables in the patch. Don't attempt to mound the soil around the bulb.

Harvest

After about 10 weeks your crop should be ready for harvest. Pull when the bulb is the size of a tennis ball: too big and they will be woody. The leaves of the plant are delicious too. Use them as you would use kale. Store in the refrigerator.

Asian kohlrabi and apple slaw

For 6 as a side dish

Peel the kohlrabi and slice it and the apple into matchsticks.

In a large bowl, combine the kohlrabi, apple, onion, oil, chilli, lemon rind and juice. Transfer to a serving bowl and scatter the herbs and nuts on top.

3 tennis ball–sized kohlrabi

1 green apple

½ red onion or 2 green onions, thinly sliced

3 tbsp extra virgin olive oil

1 green chilli, deseeded and finely chopped

Finely grated rind and juice of 1 lemon

½ cup torn coriander or parsley leaves

½ cup chopped mint leaves

½ cup crushed peanuts

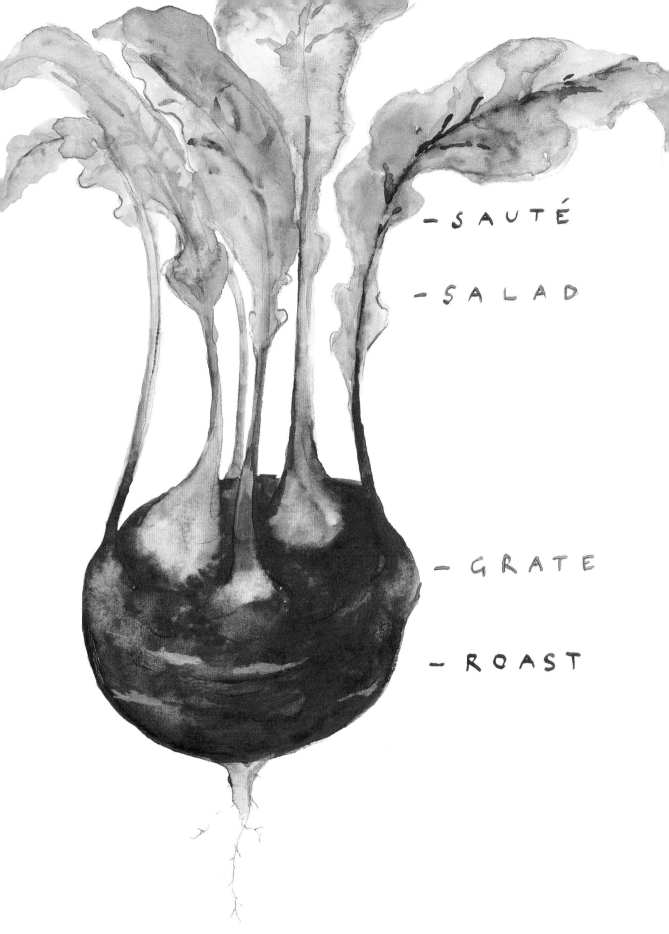

- SAUTÉ

- SALAD

- GRATE

- ROAST

Lettuce

♈	**Sow** all year
◎	**Harvest** all year
◷	**Growing time** 6–8 weeks
♥♥	**Space between plants** 15–25 cm
⊽	**Pots** yes, brilliant (large)
☼	**Aspect** full sun
⏚	**Soil pH** 5.8–7.0
✳	**Frost tolerant** yes
♡	**Companions** beetroot, carrots, parsnips, radishes, onions, broccoli
⊘	**Dislikes** celery, cress, parsley

Sow

Sow undercover or directly into the ground. Use a seed-raising mix and sprinkle the seed on top. Then cover with more mix or vermiculite grains and water carefully. Keep the seedling tray moist at all times: I use a spray bottle. Plant out when they are 5 cm tall. Sow directly into soil very well prepared with manure or all-round fertiliser. Choose a spot that has good drainage, as lettuces tend to rot if the area is too wet. Sow into rows 30 cm apart. Refer to the distancing of seeds on the seed packet as there are variations with each type of lettuce. Lettuce is a wonderful plant for balcony gardens or where there isn't much space. Plant in a large container and mix up the varieties for an attractive display.

Nurture

Keep well watered, especially in summer and liquid feed every 2 weeks. Be on the watch for slimy bugs such as snails and slugs. They love nothing more than a lettuce leaf. See p. 186 for ways to keep your lettuce snail-free.

Harvest

You can remove the outer leaves as you go rather than harvesting the whole plant. With more compact lettuces, such as iceberg, it is better to slice off the whole lettuce from the bottom.

Simple salad dressing

I read once that your salad should be like your guests ... well dressed, not overdressed!

I will change the dressing to suit whichever leaf I am using. If it is rocket, I just squeeze over the juice of a lemon, add a good pinch of flaky salt and a drizzle of extra virgin olive oil. Done. The better-quality oil you use, the better the dressing will taste.

For a butter lettuce I prefer a French salad dressing: crush a quarter of a clove of garlic with 1 teaspoon of Dijon mustard, 2 tablespoons of white wine vinegar, 125 ml (½ cup) of extra virgin olive oil, a pinch of salt and a teaspoon of honey. Whisk together and add it to your salad.

Always dress your salad just before serving.

COS

RED CORAL

FRISEE

ENDIVE

RED OAK

ARUGULA

RED ROMAINE

BUTTER

ICEBERG

CRESS

Varieties

Cos – less likely to rot, tall and crisp
Iceberg – round, compact
Butter – soft leafed
Little Gem – upright and firm

Peas

♈	**Sow** autumn, winter
◎	**Harvest** autumn, winter
◷	**Growing time** 12–14 weeks
♥♥	**Space between plants** 20 cm apart
▽	**Pots** yes
☀	**Aspect** full sun
⤓	**Soil pH** 5.8–7.0
❄	**Frost tolerant** yes
♡	**Companions** beans, cabbage, lettuce, carrots, beetroot
☉	**Dislikes** chives, garlic, onions

Varieties

Peas are available as dwarf, standard and climbing varieties.

Sugar snap – climber, long fruiting, reliable
Snow pea – climber
Novella – dwarf, no staking, prolific, very sweet
Greenfeast – standard, prolific
Early Crop Massey – dwarf, crops early

Sow

Prepare soil with compost, manure and a layer of mulch. Peas like a friable soil that drains well. Check for acidity in soil; add lime if it is too high. Soak the seeds overnight before planting. Peas can be started early in growing tubes or pods in the late winter, under cover. Keep well watered. Pea seeds and seedlings started in a greenhouse can be planted out from early spring as they can tolerate a light frost.

Sow 5 cm apart. Protect new shoots from birds, slugs and mice with cloches, nets and slug pits (beer in plastic or paper cups, see p. 186).

Nurture

Peas don't need a lot of fertiliser, just well-prepared soil. Climbing peas need a trellis or frame to climb onto, or it is possible to use a fence. They work well in rows or grouped under an obelisk-like structure. Twigs or sticks can work for a rustic look. Dwarf peas don't need staking. Keep plants well watered especially when the flowers appear. Don't allow beds to dry out.

Harvest

Once the peas are looking fat within the pods they are ready for harvesting. The more you pick, the more the plant will flower and fruit. Leave some pods to dry out on the plant to collect for seed.

PEAS

Roasted radicchio with peas, capers and tarragon cream

For 6

Adapted from Gill Meller's roast little gem and peas recipe

Preheat the oven to 200°C.

Cut thick wedges of radicchio and rub with olive oil. Lay them on a baking tray and roast for 20 minutes or until soft.

Meanwhile, in a heavy-based frying pan, melt the butter and fry the green onion, garlic and capers for 5 minutes. Add vegetable or chicken stock and peas and cook for a further 5 minutes. Add the cream and mustard and cook for another 2 minutes. Add tarragon and season with salt and pepper. Transfer radicchio to a serving platter and pour the sauce over.

1 large round radicchio lettuce
2 tbsp extra virgin olive oil
50 g butter
2 green onions, chopped
1 garlic clove, chopped
1 heaped tbsp of tiny capers
150 ml vegetable or chicken stock
100 g shelled peas (or frozen)
75 ml double cream
1 tsp Dijon mustard
1 small handful of chopped tarragon
    leaves
Salt and pepper

RADICCHIO

Radicchio

♈	**Sow** autumn
◎	**Harvest** autumn, winter
◐	**Growing time** 12–14 weeks
⚘	**Space between plants** 15–25 cm
⊟	**Pots** yes, brilliant (large)
☼	**Aspect** full sun
⌁	**Soil pH** 5.8–7.0
❋	**Frost tolerant** yes
♡	**Companions** beetroot, carrots, parsnips, radishes, onions
⊙	**Dislikes** none

Varieties

Rossa di Verona – cup shaped leaves, bitter, can be eaten cooked or raw

Sow

Sow in the cooler time of year otherwise it tends to bolt to seed. You can start undercover if you wish, but it's really better with direct sowing into well-prepared garden beds (see p. 158). Sprinkle seed into rows and thin out as the plants get bigger. For undercover sowing, use seedling mix and vermiculite as a light topping to retain moisture. Plant out at 10 cm.

Nurture

Keep well watered and fertilise with liquid feed, roughly every 2 weeks. Watch for slugs (see p. 186).

Harvest

Cut off the head of the plant and leave the rest in the ground for more to regrow.

Radicchio with anchovy dressing and fried breadcrumbs

For 6

I had this salad at Fred's in Paddington, Sydney, and couldn't believe how good it was. I left for New York City shortly afterwards and was asked to make a salad for my sister's birthday lunch, so I decided to recreate it from memory. It was served up to some of NYC's top foodies and got the big thumbs-up, so I feel this version stands up well.

1 egg
250 ml (1 cup) light extra virgin olive oil or grapeseed oil
Juice of ½ a lemon
1 tsp Dijon mustard
20 anchovies
1 cup panko breadcrumbs
Oil for frying
1 radicchio lettuce

Break the whole egg carefully into a tall jar. Place a stick blender carefully over the yolk (so the blades straddle it) and pour in the oil, lemon and mustard. Blitz and slowly pull the blender up to incorporate the oil. Add anchovies. Blitz again.

Toast the breadcrumbs in a frying pan with a small amount of oil.

Tear radicchio leaves into a large flat dish, not a deep bowl. Add the dressing and toss until well coated. Sprinkle with toasted breadcrumbs and serve immediately.

Silverbeet, chard, English spinach

- **Sow** all year
- **Harvest** spring, autumn, winter
- **Growing time** 6–12 weeks
- **Space between plants** 15–20 cm
- **Pots** yes, brilliant (large)
- **Aspect** full sun
- **Soil pH** 5.8–7.0
- **Frost tolerant** yes
- **Companions** everything except those listed below
- **Dislikes** basil

Varieties

Rainbow Chard – beautifully coloured stems
Golden Sunrise – good flavour and frost hardy
Ruby Red – good for salads or cooking

Sow

Seedlings can be started off undercover in seed trays (see p. 165). Seeds should be sown 2.5 cm deep and thinned out to small pots at 5 cm. Seeds can also be directly sown into their beds after soil preparation (see p. 158).

Use a high-nitrogen fertiliser such as chicken manure. Create drills (shallow lines in the soil made with a pointed stick or dibber) in rows at 30 cm intervals to the depth of 2.5 cm. Sow 10 cm apart and, as they grow, thin the plants to 30 cm apart.

Nurture

Liquid feed every two weeks or so. Keep the plants well watered in the hotter months.

Harvest

Plants can be harvested when the plant is young through to maturity. Snip stems near to the base to encourage regrowth.

RAINBOW CHARD

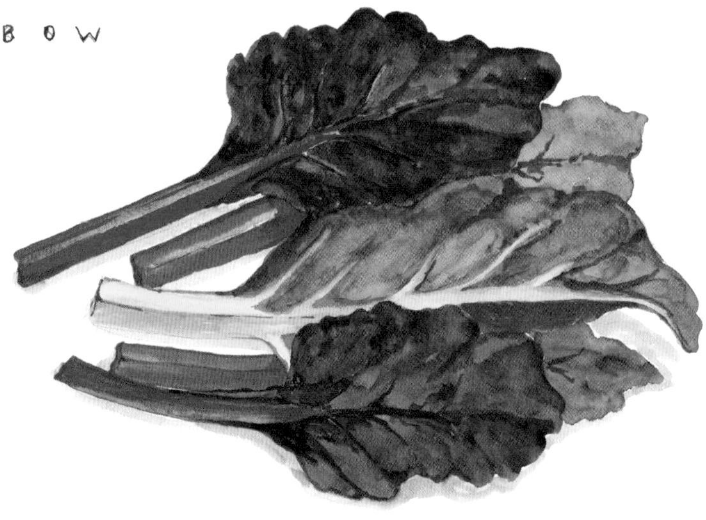

Pickled rainbow chard

Makes 2–3 medium preserving jars

Pack washed chard into sterilised glass jars along with dill and garlic (see p. 190).

Put 250 ml (1 cup) of water in a medium saucepan and add vinegar, peppercorns, mustard seeds, chilli flakes, salt and sugar. Bring to a boil and simmer until sugar and salt has dissolved.

Carefully pour the hot brine over the chard. Let jars cool to room temperature.

Seal jars and refrigerate for at least 3 hours before serving. Use within 3 months.

3 cups rainbow chard stalks, chopped
2 large sprigs of dill
1 small garlic clove, thinly sliced
250 ml (1 cup) water
250 ml (1 cup) white vinegar
1 tsp black peppercorns
1 tbsp yellow mustard seeds
½ tsp dried chilli flakes
2 tsp kosher salt or any salt
   without iodine
1 tsp granulated sugar

Swedes and turnips

♈	**Sow** late summer, autumn
◎	**Harvest** spring
◷	**Growing time** 20–24 weeks
➳➳	**Space between plants** 20 cm
☖	**Pots** no
☼	**Aspect** full sun, part shade
⏚	**Soil pH** 5.8–7.0
❋	**Frost tolerant** yes
♡	**Companions** onions, peas, beetroot, Brussels sprouts, spinach, choy sum, garlic, leeks
⌢	**Dislikes** potatoes, tomatoes, strawberries, eggplant

Varieties
Champion Purple Top – good for soups or stews
Purple Top White Globe – good flesh flavour
Hakurei – Japanese turnip with white skin, lovely flavour

Sow
Loose friable soil is best for root vegetables like swedes and turnips. Mix sand with compost and work it right through the soil. Sow seeds directly in rows approximately 5 cm apart and cover with seed-raising mix. Water in very gently. Seedlings will emerge in about a week. Thin out seedlings when they are 8 cm high leaving 15–20 cm between each plant.

Nurture
If plants aren't thriving, feed with a nitrogen-based fertiliser. They respond well to liquid feeds.

Harvest
Pull swedes and turnips when they are about the size of a cricket ball. After lifting, cut the stems off and store the globes in the fridge.

Crispy pan-fried swedes

Peel and dice swedes. Put the swede in a heavy-based frying pan and add enough stock so the swedes are half submerged. Add chunks of butter (about 50 g in total) and simmer until the stock is absorbed and the swedes start to caramelise. Season with salt and pepper.

CRISPY PAN FRIED SWEDES

Chapter 04

Winter planting

I've heard gardeners say they love winter gardens. It's a time to see the bare bones and to rethink certain parts of the garden. For the winter vegetable garden, it is really a race to get the winter-hardy vegetables to a certain size before it gets too cold, so that they can keep feeding you throughout winter. The planting of anything in the middle to late months of winter doesn't result in much for people in the cold or even temperate zones. So, if you want full vegetable beds, start them in mid-autumn. Flowers such as pansies, violas and violets are pretty winter additions to your vegetable patch. Even though growth can be slow in winter, it's still worth having a few bunches of silverbeet, beetroot, broad beans and parsnips on the go. Some gardeners like to plant out green manure crops (a mixture of legumes) at this time to push nitrogen back into the soil, especially after hungry crops such as tomatoes. There are always a few hours in the day that are enjoyable to be out in the garden in winter, but the nicest part is taking your boots off and coming in to sit in front of the fire.

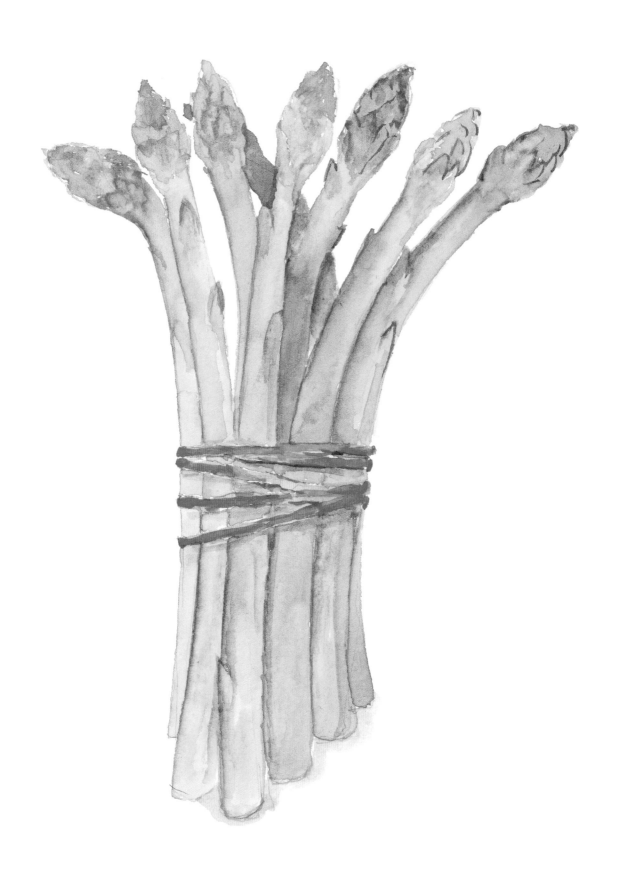

Asparagus

♈	**Sow** winter
◎	**Harvest** spring
☉	**Growing time** first crop 2–3 years
♥♥	**Space between plants** 35 cm
⊽	**Pots** no
☼	**Aspect** full sun
⚖	**Soil pH** 5.8–7.0
✳	**Frost tolerant** yes
♡	**Companions** carrots, basil, tomatoes, eggplant, dill
⊘	**Dislikes** garlic, onions, potatoes

Varieties
Jersey Giant – popular
Mary Washington – early sprouting
Sweet Purple – plum-coloured spears

Sow
Start with 'bare-root crowns' (often found in a garden centre, or transplant from a friend's garden) rather than starting with seeds as they take *way* too long to get to the crop stage. Prepare the soil and make sure it is cultivated to the depth of at least 20 cm with a well-rotted manure.

Create a trench to the depth of 15 cm. Plant the crowns 30 cm apart with the crown facing upwards. Cover and water in well.

Nurture
Fertilise in late winter just before crowns appear above the soil. Water well in the summer months.

Cut the fern to the ground in autumn when the plants turn yellow. Add a thick layer of mulch.

Harvest
The spears need to be left for the first 2 years to allow the plant to mature to crop stage. Once your crop has reached maturity you can harvest the spears when they get to about 20 cm tall. The asparagus tends to grow extremely fast and needs picking daily. Cut the spears below the soil line with a sharp knife. In early summer, stop harvesting and allow the spears to develop into ferns. Leave them throughout summer to bulk up and recover, putting nutrients back into the crowns.

Simple asparagus

Bring a large saucepan of salted water to the boil. Meanwhile, prepare a large bunch of asparagus by cutting off the woody ends. Drop asparagus into the boiling water for 5 minutes or until al dente. Whisk one lemon, a good pinch of flaky salt, a grind of pepper and 80 ml (⅓ cup) of extra virgin olive oil (the better the quality the better it will taste). Drizzle over the asparagus and shave some parmesan cheese on top.

Blackberries

Sow winter, spring

Harvest summer, autumn

Growing time 6–8 weeks

Space between plants 1.5–3 m

Pots no

Aspect full sun

Soil pH 6.8–7.5

Frost tolerant yes

Companions peas, beans

Dislikes tomatoes, potatoes, eggplant, capsicums, strawberries

Varieties
Silvanberry – early summer, large fruit
Loganberry – sharp in taste
Tayberry – cross raspberry and blackberry
Boysenberry – cross loganberry and blackberry

Sow
There are many hybrid varieties that are suited to the modern garden, with fewer thorns and more fruit, which makes them a joy to have in the vegetable garden. Choose a large fence, trellis or wall to grow your canes on. Tie your canes in a fan shape. Prepare your soil (see p. 158). Canes should be planted at least 1.5–3 metres apart.

Nurture
Use mulch generously to keep your plants from drying out. They don't need extra fertiliser if the soil has been prepared well before planting. They will most probably need netting to protect the berries from birds, but this can be difficult if there are thorns. Canes that have fruited can be cut down to the ground in winter while newer non-fruiting canes can be left and tied to the trellis to bear next season's fruit.

Harvest
Pick fruit as it ripens.

Summer pudding

For 8

I remember my mother used to make this when I was a child in the seventies. It took centre stage at many of her dinner parties. How could white bread soaked in berry juice taste so good? Well, it just does.

Find a 2 litre pudding bowl and line it carefully with white bread without crusts. The more care you take in this bit the better. My mother used to use scissors to first cut a shape for the bottom of the bowl, then work her way around the edges slightly overlapping each piece.

Put approximately 1.2 kg of mixed berries (blackberries, raspberries, loganberries, strawberries and blueberries... variety is important) in a big saucepan. Add 350 g of caster sugar and heat on low, carefully turning over the fruit as you go. After about 6–7 minutes strain the fruit and reserve both fruit and juice.

Gently remove the pieces of bread from the pudding bowl and use a pastry brush to dab on the juices from the berries. Reline the bowl, putting the juice side against the bowl.

Spoon the berries into the bread-lined bowl. Make a bread lid on top. Pour in all the berry juice. Use a small plate to cover the top of the pudding and weigh it down with something heavy so the pudding is compressed. Refrigerate for 24 hours, before turning out onto a plate for serving with thick cream.

Blueberries

♈	**Sow** winter, spring
◎	**Harvest** summer, autumn
◷	**Growing time** 8–10 weeks
᪥	**Space between plants** 75 cm
▽	**Pots** yes
☼	**Aspect** full sun
⬇	**Soil pH** 4.0–5.0
❄	**Frost tolerant** yes
♡	**Companions** basil, thyme, rhubarb
⊙	**Dislikes** Blueberries prefer an acidic soil, so any plants that like a pH above 6 won't be a good companion.

Varieties
Brightwell – sweet, high yield
Sharpblue – high yield
Bluecrop – deciduous, sweet

Sow
Plant in the winter for a summer crop, spacing plants around 75 cm apart. While blueberries are self-fertile, co-planting more than one variety will help improve pollination and yield. You can buy blueberry plants in pots.

Test your soil to check the soil acidity. Blueberries need a pH reading between 4 and 5. If it is higher than that, add granular sulphur to the soil (this is best added a few months prior to planting). Till into the soil and water in. Used coffee grounds are a good addition. Add compost and manure and use mulch to cover.

Nurture
Feed your blueberries in spring with an azalea fertiliser. Keep your patch well-watered. Remove any dead or diseased branches before the plant comes into leaf in spring. Reduce all the branches by a third to two-thirds if it has reached its full height (usually after 4 years).

Harvest
Leave fruit until fully ripe, as it won't continue to ripen once picked.

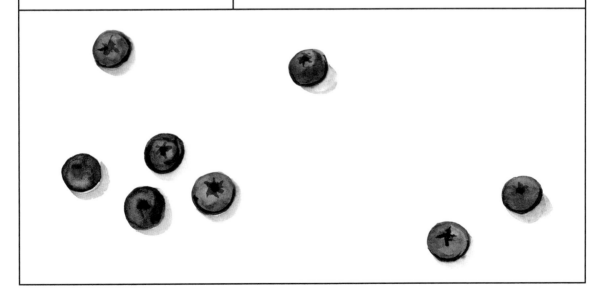

Blueberry and almond cake

For 8

Preheat the oven to 180°C. Grease and line a 22 cm cake tin.

Mix dry ingredients in a mixing bowl with a whisk.

In a separate bowl, beat together the sugar and eggs with an electric beater on medium for five minutes until the mixture becomes pale and increases in volume. While the mixer is still running slowly, pour in the melted butter and oil. Add the almond extract. It should look thick and glossy.

Fold in dry ingredients and the blueberries and pour into your cake tin.

Bake for 35–40 mins. Poke a skewer into the cake and if it comes out clean it's ready.

Let the cake cool before turning it out onto a cake plate. Dust with icing sugar and serve with thick cream.

4 eggs, lightly beaten
200 g sugar
50 g vegetable oil
70 g butter, melted
1 tsp almond extract
375 g blueberries (you can use frozen)
Icing sugar, for dusting
Thick cream, to serve (optional)

Dry ingredients
170 g almond flour
85 g all-purpose flour
½ tsp baking powder
½ tsp salt

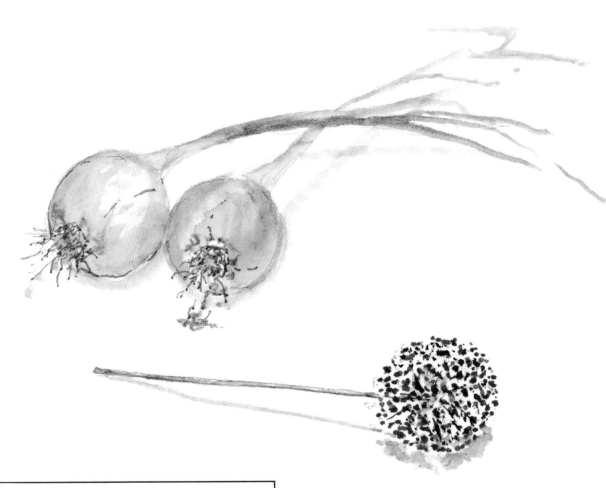

There are many varieties of onions. Chives and
spring, green and red onions are mostly used raw
whereas eschalots and white, brown and yellow
onions are generally used in cooking.

Varieties
Barletta – salad onion
Cream Gold – brown, excellent storing ability
Red Odourless – good red onion
Sweet Red – good raw onion

Onions

♈	**Sow** autumn, winter
◎	**Harvest** spring, summer, autumn
🕐	**Growing time** 20–24 weeks
♈♈	**Space between plants** 10 cm
🪴	**Pots** possible
☀	**Aspect** full sun
⏚	**Soil pH** 6.8–7.5
✳	**Frost tolerant** yes
♡	**Companions** everything except those listed below
⊙	**Dislikes** beans, broad beans, peas

Sow

Sow in trays with seedling mix and cover sprinkled seeds with a fine layer of soil and vermiculite grains. It's difficult to create spacing at this stage, but once your seedlings are 10 cm high you can easily thin them out. Plant out at 10 cm intervals.

Direct sow into garden beds and thin out if there is crowding. Each plant needs space to grow to maturity. Keep well-watered.

Nurture

You will need to keep your onion patch well weeded as onions don't like to compete. Apply a high-nitrogen fertiliser at the end of winter to get good-sized summer crops. Onions are good self-sowers so leave some plants to flower and do their thing. The dried onion flower is rather beautiful. I secure a paper bag over the flower and hang it upside down until it dries off and drops all its seeds. Keep the dried flower for arranging.

Harvest

Pull onions when they get to the desired size (usually when the tops are dying back). If the soil is compacted, use a garden fork to loosen and extract the onions. Dry the onions in the greenhouse for a week or so. When the skins are dry store in an airy dry place in net bags or baskets.

Pissaladière

For 6

Preheat the oven to 210°C. Slice 3–4 large onions and gently fry in olive oil until they are golden in colour and become very soft. This should be done slowly and gently. Roll out 375 g of puff pastry into a large rectangle, or use 2 layers of frozen pastry sheets to double the thickness. Lay the pastry on a lightly floured baking tray and spread the onions onto the pastry, leaving a 1 cm border. Lay anchovies (you will need at least one small jar) diagonally across the onion to create a diamond or lattice pattern. Bake for 30 minutes or until golden brown.

Raspberries

♈	**Sow** winter
◎	**Harvest** summer, autumn
◷	**Growing time** 6–8 weeks
⚊⚊	**Space between plants** 30 cm
⛻	**Pots** yes
☀	**Aspect** full sun
⬍	**Soil pH** 6.8–7.5
❋	**Frost tolerant** no
♡	**Companions** garlic, chives, nasturtiums, leeks
⊙	**Dislikes** tomatoes, eggplant, potatoes

Varieties
Heritage – autumn fruit
Willamette – dual season fruit, high yield
Chilliwack – midsummer, popular

Sow
Purchase bare-root plants from fellow gardeners or your local nursery. There are two types of raspberries: summer fruiting and autumn. They require different types of pruning, so you will need to identify the canes, either by separation or labelling. Choose a sunny spot and cultivate the garden soil (see p. 158). Raspberries like moist but free-draining soil. Plant the canes at intervals of 30 cm and rows 1 metre apart. Create a trellis that has two horizontal wires, one at 50 cm and the other at 1 metre from the ground. Secure the canes as they grow. Mulch well to retain moisture.

Nurture
Keep the plants well-watered and feed with a tomato fertiliser at the beginning of spring. Raspberries need protection from birds (or in my case, my dog). Netting is the best way to protect them.

Autumn raspberries bear fruit on both first-year canes (primocanes) and subsequent floricanes while summer raspberries only bear fruit on the floricanes. Autumn raspberries are prolific in autumn with a possible next crop in the early summer. However, summer raspberries fruit only in the summer.

If you have autumn raspberries you can cut all the canes close to the ground in winter.

If you have summer raspberries you can cut the canes that have fruited to the ground and reduce the size of the non-fruiting canes to the height of the first wire.

Harvest
Harvest fruit carefully when the berries are dark red. Picking fruit regularly increases your yield.

R A S P B E R R Y J A M

Raspberry jam

Makes 8 small preserving jars

I can't keep up with the demand for raspberry jam in my little shop, The Mud Room. The recipe is simple.

2 kg raspberries
2 kg sugar
Juice of 2 lemons

Put 2 small saucers in the freezer for testing (see p. 190). In a large saucepan, boil all the ingredients gently for 20 minutes, stirring often. Test the jam by dropping a small amount of jam on a very cold saucer. It will quickly become jam-like if it is cooked. If it's too runny, keep cooking and test every 5 minutes. I don't use jam setters, but you can if you prefer a very jelly-like consistency. I actually prefer it to be a little loose. Pour the jam into hot sterilised jars and set aside to cool to room temperature (see p. 190). Seal with the lids and store in a cool dark place for up to 6 months.

Strawberries

♈	**Sow** winter, spring
◎	**Harvest** spring, summer, autumn
🕐	**Growing time** 2–4 weeks
♥♥	**Space between plants** 30 cm
🪴	**Pots** yes
☼	**Aspect** full sun
⊥	**Soil pH** 6.8–7.5
✳	**Frost tolerant** yes
♡	**Companions** lettuce, chives, sage, carrots
⊙	**Dislikes** tomatoes, eggplant, potatoes, roses

Varieties
Albion – popular, sweet
Juliette – Australian bred, large, sweet
Cambridge Rival – good yield

Sow
It's good to grow a few varieties of strawberries, as each will bear fruit depending on the conditions. Some are long fruiting, some early and some late. Prepare your strawberry beds by cultivating the soil with compost and manure. The plants are available bare-rooted or in a pot. Choose a sunny spot in the garden. Plant out with 30 cm between each plant. Mulching is essential as it stops the bed from drying out, but more importantly it keeps the fruit from spoiling by lifting it off the soil. Mulch in the form of black plastic is often used. I use torn up cardboard with straw on top. Strawberries grow well in pots.

Nurture
Net beds to protect from birds who love to snack on strawberries. Water regularly as strawberries need moisture to fruit. A drip system under the mulch works best as it won't spoil the fruit. If fruit is poor, cut back the runners and this should stimulate a new crop.

Harvest
Pick strawberries when they are dark red. The plants will give more fruit the more you pick.

Dehydrated strawberries

Preheat the oven to 90°C. Wash and dry 500 g of strawberries. Hull and carefully slice into 3 mm thick slices and lay them on a baking tray lined with baking paper. Bake for 2 hours or until they feel dry. Then peel them off the paper, turn them over and bake for a further 30 minutes until fully dehydrated. Store in an airtight jar in the pantry for up to 6 months. They are delicious in salads and as a snack.

Chapter 05

Growing fruit trees

Growing fruit shouldn't be overlooked in the smaller kitchen garden. Dwarf varieties of fruit trees are available and are great in pots. Citrus trees, especially lemons, are a must if your climate allows you to grow them. I compete heavily with the birds for my fruit trees. I have a deal with them: they can have the top fruit and I'll take the bottom! This mostly works. I feel that both they and I have an eagle eye for the point of ripeness. Fruit growing is essential to the home preserver. Fruit preserved properly can be stored for up to a year. I love that I can open a bottle of quinces at any time of the year and serve it simply with cream as a delicious dessert, or turn the fruit into an impressive tart. If I have an abundance of fruit for bottling I invite like-minded friends around to give me a hand. We happily sit in the kitchen and peel, slice, stir and chat. Everyone goes home with jars of goodness.

Apples

♈	**Plant** winter
◎	**Harvest** summer
◷	**Growing time** 14–20 weeks
♈♈	**Space between plants** 3 m
⛉	**Pots** yes
☀	**Aspect** full sun
⚓	**Soil pH** 5.5–7.5
❋	**Frost tolerant** yes

Varieties

There are lots of varieties when it comes to apples, so check with your local nursery about suitable ones for you.

Apples for baking:
Jonagold, Braeburn, Pink Lady, Granny Smith

Apples for eating:
Red Delicious, Fuji, Golden Delicious, Pink Lady, Gala

Plant

You will need two trees so that they can cross-pollinate. Or have one nearby with a neighbour.

Young trees can be bought in pots ready to plant. Dig a large hole and cultivate the soil with well-rotted manure (or an all-round fertiliser) and compost. Pull the tree from its pot and gently tickle the roots to loosen. Lower into the hole so the soil level matches the bottom of the tree. Backfill the hole with soil. Stake either side with two stakes and some soft twine.

Dwarf varieties can be grown in pots.

Nurture

Water your young tree regularly, especially in the first year when it's establishing its roots. Once established it doesn't require a lot of water, but it is good to give your tree a deep watering in the hottest part of summer. It is wise to compost around the base of the tree in spring and to add manure and top with mulch to keep the area from drying off.

If you have lots of fruit it is important to thin the fruit out so the weight doesn't drag the branches down too much. Prune trees by creating a shape similar to a wine glass. Ideally there should be outer branches cupped around a hollow centre. This creates airflow and therefore reduces the chance of disease. Any crossover branches that are touching should be removed.

Harvest

Apples are ready to pick when you are able to hold the fruit, gently push up and twist and it comes away easily. Apples store well for months in a cool place.

Apple and ginger cake

For 6

Preheat the oven to 180°C. Grease and line a 22 cm cake tin.

Melt 100 g butter and half the sugar in a fry pan until combined. Add the apple and fry on low for about 10 minutes until soft. Transfer the apple mixture to the cake tin and arrange the apple evenly.

In a mixing bowl, sift in the flour, bicarb soda, ginger and cinnamon and set aside. In an electric mixer (on medium speed) beat the remaining butter with the remaining sugar until pale and creamy. Add the treacle, then the eggs, one by one. Beat well in between. Now slowly add the dry mix you prepared earlier, alternating with the buttermilk. Pour mixture over the apples and bake for 55 minutes or until the cake returns a clean skewer when tested.

Serve with cream or ice cream.

225 g butter (preferably room temperature)

250 g dark brown sugar

4 apples, peeled, cored and diced into big chunks

450 g plain flour

1 tsp bicarb soda

2 tbsp ground ginger

2 tsp ground cinnamon

370 g treacle

3 eggs

250 g buttermilk

Pouring cream or ice cream, to serve (optional)

Cherries

♈	**Plant** winter
◎	**Harvest** summer
◷	**Growing time** 10–14 weeks
☙☙	**Space between plants** 3–4 m
⊽	**Pots** no
☀	**Aspect** full sun
⇩	**Soil pH** 6.0–6.5
❊	**Frost tolerant** yes

Varieties
Bing – sweet, dark flesh, need more than one tree
Morello – sour, light flesh
Lapins – dark, large fruit, good for jam

Plant
Cherry trees are best planted in pairs to pollinate; however, some varieties are self-pollinators, so you need to check this when you are selecting your tree.

Trees are best planted bare-rooted in winter when the tree is dormant. Cherries can be bought in pots ready to plant. Dig a large hole and cultivate the soil with well-rotted manure (or an all-round fertiliser) and compost. Pull the tree from its pot and gently tickle the roots to loosen. Lower into the hole so the soil level matches the bottom of the tree. Backfill the hole with soil. Hammer in two wooden stakes either side of the tree, outside the root line. Use soft stretchy twine to tie the tree in place. This will protect it from being knocked. You can also wrap chicken wire or use agricultural plastic sleeves if you are in a rural area and animals are a risk.

Nurture
Keep young trees well watered. Keep the root area well mulched. Early spring is a good time to add fertiliser and compost. Apply an all-round fertiliser in spring followed by a high-potassium (potash) fertiliser at the beginning of summer. I use a tomato fertiliser from my local garden supplier. Prune cherry trees after fruiting while they are still in leaf. Cut long lengths back to the next branch.

Harvest
Harvest cherries when ripe and store them in the fridge.

Cherry jam
1 kg of fruit makes 4 small preserving jars

Wash the fruit and cut out pips; you can buy a cherry pipper which makes it easier. Weigh the fruit. Put fruit in a large saucepan and weigh out an equal amount of sugar to add to the cherries. This recipe is essentially half sugar and half fruit, so whatever your cherries weigh, you should use the same amount of sugar. Squeeze in the juice of one lemon for every 1 kg of fruit. Boil for 10 minutes, then check to see if your jam has set using the method on p. 190. Once ready, transfer to sterilised jars (see p. 190) and seal.

Varieties

ORANGES

Valencia – sweet summer
variety, good for juicing,
fast growing

Navel – winter fruiters

Seville – bitter and make a
superior marmalade

LEMONS

Eureka – tangy, not frost
tolerant, thornless

Meyer – sweet, smooth skinned,
best in frosty areas

Lisbon – thorny, fast growing
and frost tolerant

LIMES

Key lime – fruit turns from green
to yellow, tart, juicy

Desert lime – Australian native,
good for cooking

Finger lime – Australian native,
caviar-like flesh, zingy

Citrus

♈	**Plant** spring
◎	**Harvest** all year
◷	**Growing time** 10 weeks
♈♈	**Space between plants** 3 m
⬚	**Pots** yes
☼	**Aspect** sun
⏚	**Soil pH** 5.5–7.5
✳	**Frost tolerant** Lemons are generally not frost tolerant; however, varieties such as Meyer lemons will tolerate light frosts. Oranges and limes are frost tolerant.

Plant

Spring is the best time to plant your citrus tree. It is important to choose the right variety of citrus for your area as some are more frost tolerant than others. Find a sunny spot that is protected from wind. Young trees can be bought in pots ready to plant. Dig a large hole and cultivate the soil with well-rotted manure (or an all-round fertiliser) and compost. Pull the tree from its pot and gently tickle the roots to loosen. Lower into the hole so the soil level matches the bottom of the tree. Backfill the hole with soil.

Nurture

Citrus trees are hungry and thirsty. Apply citrus food high in blood and bone in spring and summer.

Watering regularly is necessary in the warmer months, especially with trees in containers. Gall wasps are the biggest problem with citrus trees, and they tend to attack trees that aren't healthy. Snip off any obvious bulging sections where the wasps have laid their eggs. These prunings must be burnt or disposed of by putting them in a plastic bag and leaving in the sun to solarise.

Leaf miners can be treated with neem oil (see p. 187).

Prune in spring if you are trying to shape. You can cut growth back by one-third, especially if the tree is unhealthy. They spring back enthusiastically.

Harvest

Most citrus can be harvested in winter. The fruit should easily twist off the branch. Limes and lemons ripen periodically and can be harvested all year.

Orange slices with toffee

For 6

This recipe comes from my childhood and I'm not sure of the origins. It is the most refreshing and pretty dessert. The crunchy toffee sits drizzled on the slices of oranges and the juice of the oranges somehow becomes almost caramelised in taste. It's especially good served straight from the fridge.

Peel and slice the oranges. Arrange slices in a single layer, slightly overlapping, on a large plate. Put it in the fridge (this part can be done ahead of time).

Stir the sugar and water in a saucepan over high heat. When it looks a lovely golden colour, remove from the heat and drizzle the syrup over the oranges. Set aside for a while so the flavours mesh.

10 oranges
1 cup sugar
60 ml (¼ cup) water

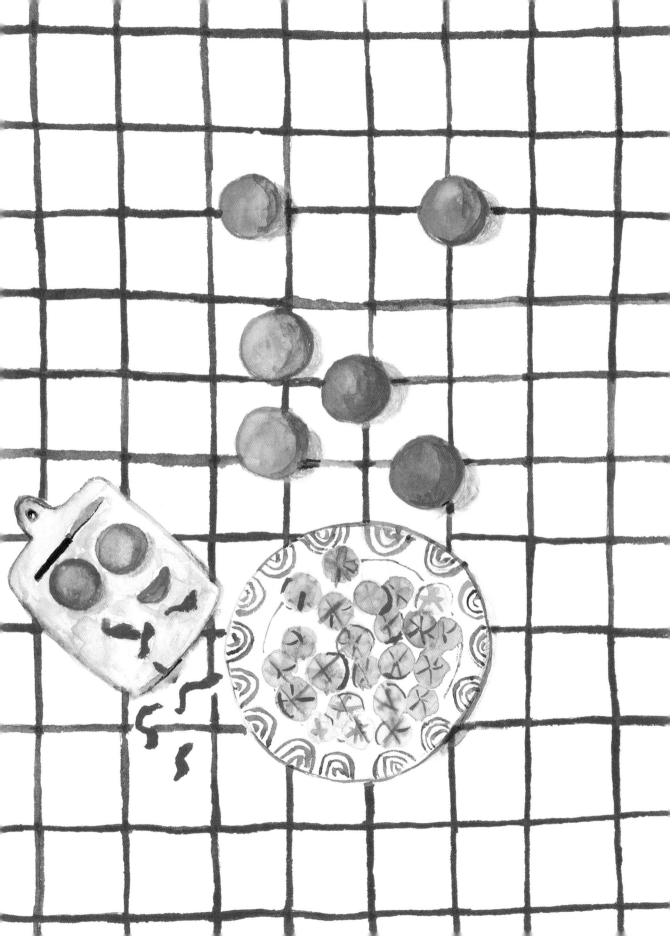

Crabapples

♈	**Plant** winter
◎	**Harvest** summer
☉	**Growing time** 14–20 weeks
⚇	**Space between plants** 3 m
▽	**Pots** yes
☀	**Aspect** sun
⚓	**Soil pH** 5.5–7.5
✳	**Frost tolerant** yes

Varieties

Mostly crabapples are bought for their very beautiful flower or the colour of their fruit however some varieties are better for jelly. There are many varieties available, here are a few:

Malus Dolgo – beautiful large fruit, early ripening, high in pectin
Malus John Downie – can be eaten raw or cooked, red fruit
Malus Golden Hornet – pretty yellow fruit, lighter coloured jelly

Plant

You will need two trees so that they can cross-pollinate. Or have one nearby with a neighbour.

Young trees can be bought in pots ready to plant. Dig a large hole and cultivate the soil with well-rotted manure (or an all-round fertiliser) and compost. Pull the tree from its pot and gently tickle the roots to loosen. Lower into the hole so the soil level matches the bottom of the tree. Backfill the hole with soil. Stake either side with two stakes and some soft twine.

Nurture

Water young trees regularly, especially in the first year when they're establishing roots. Once established the tree doesn't require a lot of water, but it is good to give your tree a deep watering in the hottest part of summer. It is wise to compost around the base of the tree in spring and to add manure and top with mulch to keep the area from drying off.

CRABAPPLE JELLY

Crabapple jelly

Makes 2 small preserving jars

Put the crabapples in a large saucepan, just cover with water and add the lemon rind. Bring to the boil and simmer for 30 minutes or until the crabapples are soft. Break up the fruit with the back of a wooden spoon.

Strain through a colander lined with muslin into a clean saucepan. This can take several hours: don't be tempted to push it through. Discarded fruit pulp can be composted.

Add 1 cup of sugar for each cup of juice. Add half the lemon juice (keep the remaining juice to use later). Put the saucepan over medium heat and gradually bring the mixture to the boil, ensuring that the sugar has completely dissolved before boiling point is reached.

Boil till the setting point is reached (test by putting a teaspoonful of liquid onto a cold saucer: see p. 190). Pour into warm sterilised jars (see p. 190) and seal with the lids. Jelly can be kept in the pantry for up to 6 months.

1.5 kg crabapples, washed and halved

1 lemon, rind pared, juiced

450 g granulated sugar (depending on how much juice is made)

A jelly bag or muslin cloth

Figs

⚘	**Plant** autumn, winter
◎	**Harvest** autumn
◔	**Growing time** 32–40 weeks
⚘⚘	**Space between plants** 3 m
⊽	**Pots** yes
☼	**Aspect** full sun
⬦	**Soil pH** 5.5–6.5
❋	**Frost tolerant** yes

Varieties
Brunswick – large, sweet
Brown Turkey – popular
Sierra – green skin

Plant
Trees are best planted bare-rooted in winter when the tree is dormant. Young trees can be bought in pots ready to plant. Dig a large hole and cultivate the soil with well-rotted manure (or an all-round fertiliser) and compost. Pull the tree from its pot and gently tickle the roots to loosen. Lower into the hole so the soil level matches the bottom of the tree. Backfill the hole with soil. Hammer in two wood stakes either side of the tree outside the root line and secure with soft ties.

Nurture
Water young trees regularly especially in the first year when they're establishing roots. When established, it doesn't require a lot of water, but it is good to give your tree deep watering in the hottest part of summer.

Harvest
Harvest when the fruit is soft and ripe.

Fig panzanella salad

For 6

Preheat the oven to 200°C. Toss the torn sourdough in a tablespoon of oil. Either grill or fry in a pan for about 8 minutes until golden and crunchy.

Place the halved figs on a baking tray with half the balsamic vinegar and the honey drizzled on top. Bake until soft.

Put the radicchio, rocket and bread in a mixing bowl and toss with the remaining oil and balsamic vinegar. Spread the radicchio mixture on a platter and lace with prosciutto, goat's cheese and figs. Drizzle with a little more oil and season with salt and pepper.

6 figs, halved
4 slices sourdough bread, torn
100 ml extra virgin olive oil
80 ml (⅓ cup) balsamic vinegar
2 tbsp honey
1 small radicchio lettuce, torn
A handful of rocket leaves
8 slices prosciutto
150 g goat's cheese or feta
Salt and pepper

Medlar

♇	**Plant** all year
◎	**Harvest** autumn, winter
◔	**Growing time** 16–20 weeks
❦❦	**Space between plants** 5 m
▽	**Pots** yes
☀	**Aspect** sun
⊥	**Soil pH** 5.5–7.5
✳	**Frost tolerant** yes

Plant
Young grafted trees can be bought in pots ready to plant. Dig a large hole and cultivate the soil with well-rotted manure (or an all-round fertiliser) and compost. Pull the tree from its pot and gently tickle the roots to loosen. Lower into the hole so the soil level matches the bottom of the tree. Backfill the hole with soil.

Nurture
Water young trees regularly, especially in the first year when roots are bedding in. Once established it doesn't require a lot of water, but water your tree deeply in the hottest part of summer. Compost around the base of the tree, add manure and top with mulch to keep the area from drying off. These trees really don't need a lot of attention.

Harvest
Harvest when fruit has softened, after frosts. They can be picked earlier and ripened inside. When the fruit goes very mushy and dark — called 'bletting' — it is ripe for use.

Medlar and caramelised pecan tart

For 8

The rotting of medlars sounds pretty unappealing, but that is when the sweetness comes out. This process is called bletting. After picking, leave the fruit in a cool place, in a single layer, until the skins turn wrinkly and the fruit is soft.

To make the pastry, process flour, sugar, butter and a pinch of salt in a food processor until mixture resembles crumbs. Add 1 teaspoon of iced water, egg yolk and lemon juice, and pulse until mixture just comes together. Turn out onto a lightly floured work surface, then shape into a disc, wrap in plastic wrap and refrigerate for 30 minutes.

Lightly grease a 23 cm pie dish. Dust your work surface with extra flour, then roll the pastry out to a 31 cm round. Trim edges, lay it over the pie dish, then press to line base of dish. Fold any overhanging pastry back onto the rim to form a double crust and crimp the edges using a fork. Refrigerate for 15 minutes to firm.

Preheat the oven to 200°C. Line the pastry with baking paper and fill with pastry weights or rice. Blind bake for 15 minutes, then remove the weights and paper, cover the edge of the pastry shell with foil to prevent browning and bake for a further 10 minutes or until the pastry is dry and golden. Remove from the oven, remove foil and cool slightly.

To make the filling, remove the skins and pips from medlars and push through a sieve.

Using an electric mixer, beat the eggs, butter, maple syrup, vanilla paste and spices on high speed for 3 minutes or until pale. Add condensed milk and medlar puree, and beat on low to medium speed until well combined. Pour mixture into pastry case and bake for 15 minutes. Reduce heat to 180°C and cook for a further 50 minutes or until almost set in the centre. Cover edges with foil if they are getting too brown.

Meanwhile, to make the pecan topping, combine all of the ingredients in a bowl. Remove the pie from the oven, add the pecan topping and bake for a further 10 minutes or until the top is caramelised. Cool before serving with a dollop of cream.

Pastry
200 g (1⅓ cups) plain flour, plus extra for dusting

1 tbsp caster sugar

150 g cold unsalted butter

Salt

1 tsp iced water

1 egg yolk

1 tsp lemon juice

Filling
450 g bletted medlars (to give 300 g puree)

4 eggs, lightly beaten

150 g butter

2 tbsp maple syrup

½ tsp vanilla paste

1 tsp ground ginger

1 tsp ground cinnamon

½ tsp ground nutmeg

375 ml (1½ cups) sweetened condensed milk

Pecan topping
75 g (⅓ cup firmly packed) brown sugar

80 g pecans

60 g butter, at room temperature

Cream, to serve

P E A R

Pears

♈	**Plant** winter
◎	**Harvest** summer, autumn
◷	**Growing time** 16–20 weeks
♈♈	**Space between plants** 3–4 m
⊽	**Pots** yes
☼	**Aspect** full sun
⬇	**Soil pH** 6.0–6.5
✳	**Frost tolerant** yes

Varieties
Winter Cole – crops in autumn
Doyenne du Comice – fruits mid-autumn
Nashi – round, sweet

Plant
Pear trees are best planted in pairs to pollinate. They are suitable for pots and they look great when espaliered.

For best results, plant your bare-rooted pear trees in winter when the tree is dormant. Pears can be bought grafted in pots ready to plant. Dig a large hole and cultivate the soil with well-rotted manure (or an all-round fertiliser) and compost. Pull the tree from its pot and gently tickle the roots to loosen. Lower into the hole so the soil level matches the bottom of the tree. Backfill the hole with soil. Hammer in two wooden stakes either side of the tree outside the root line. Use soft stretchy twine to tie the tree in place. This will protect it from being knocked. You can also wrap chicken wire around it if small animals are a risk.

Nurture
Mulch around the bottom of the tree to help keep the tree roots cool and moist. Water in hot dry spells. Fertilise the tree with a general fertiliser and a potash feed in summer. Your tree might need netting to protect from birds (see p. 186). Prune in autumn. Remove any crossover branches and anything that looks dead. The tree should have airflow within the centre and be open in shape and not congested. Lateral branches can be reduced to encourage fruiting spurs.

Harvest
Fruit is picked unripe to ripen once picked. Fruit will come away from the branch easily when it is ready.

Pear tart

For 6

Preheat the oven to 200°C. Turn the pastry onto a lightly floured surface. Using a lightly floured rolling pin, roll out to 3 mm thick. Line a 20 cm fluted pie tin with the pastry, trimming off any excess pastry. Prick the base with a fork. Line the inside of the pastry case with baking paper. Blind bake (cover the base with pastry weights or rice) for 10 minutes.

Reduce the oven temperature to 180°C. In a bowl, beat the caster sugar, butter and ground almonds using an electric handmixer for 1–2 minutes until pale and creamy. Add the egg and beat well. Add the flour and half the liqueur and beat until just combined.

Spoon the almond mixture into pastry case and smooth the surface. Thinly slice the pears and arrange on top, slightly overlapping. Gently press into the almond mixture. Bake for 20–25 minutes or until golden and the almond mixture is firm to the touch. Set aside for 10 minutes to cool slightly.

Combine the warmed jam and the remaining liqueur in a bowl. Brush the tarts with the jam mixture and serve with double cream.

250 g shortcrust pastry, homemade or frozen

100 g caster sugar

100 g unsalted butter, at room temperature

100 g ground almonds

1 egg

3 tbsp plain flour

25 ml hazelnut liqueur (optional)

4 pears peeled, cored and sliced in half

2–3 tbsp apricot jam, warmed until bubbling

Double cream, to serve

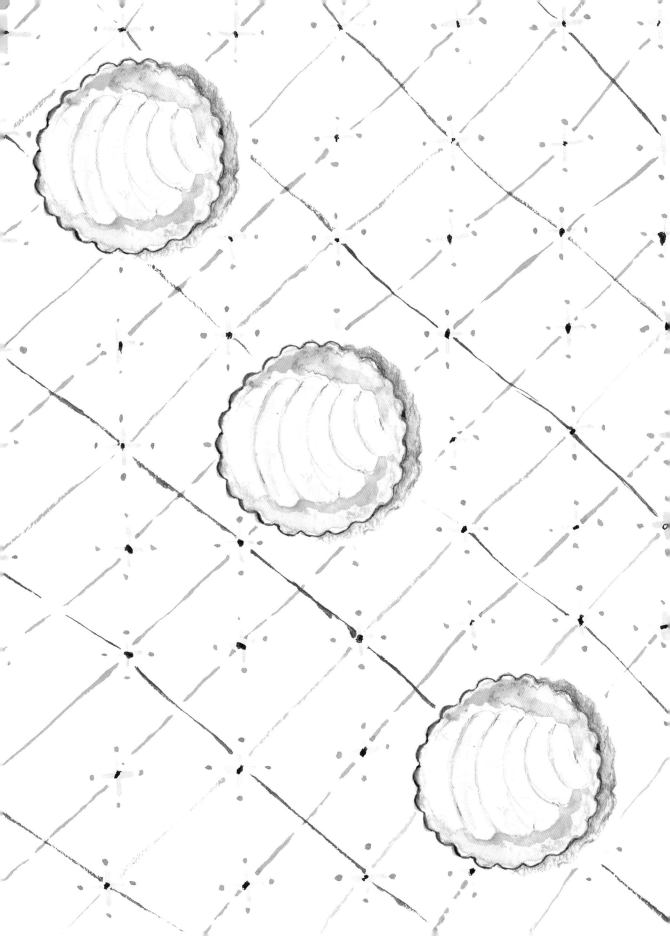

Plums

♈	**Plant** winter	
◎	**Harvest** summer, autumn	
◷	**Growing time** 14–20 weeks	
♈♈	**Space between plants** 3–4 m	
⛉	**Pots** yes	
☀	**Aspect** full sun	
⚖	**Soil pH** 6.5	
❋	**Frost tolerant** yes	

Varieties

D'Agen – yellow flesh, good for prunes
Damson plum – sharp, good for cooking
Mirabelle plum – yellow skin, small cherry size
Satsuma blood plum – good eating, sweet

Plant

Plum trees are best planted in pairs to pollinate.

Trees are best planted bare-rooted in winter when the tree is dormant. Plums can be bought grafted in pots ready to plant. Dig a large hole and cultivate the soil with well-rotted manure (or an all-round fertiliser) and compost. Pull the tree from its pot and gently tickle the roots to loosen. Lower into the hole so the soil level matches the bottom of the tree. Backfill the soil in the hole. Hammer in two wooden stakes either side of the tree outside the root line. Use soft stretchy twine to tie the tree in place. This will protect it from being knocked. You can also wrap chicken wire around if you are in a rural area and animals are a risk.

Nurture

Mulch around the bottom of the tree to help keep the tree roots cool and moist. Water during hot dry spells. Fertilise the tree with a fertiliser high in nitrogen and a general fertiliser in summer. Your tree might need netting to protect from birds. Reduce congested growth and dead branches. Prune to create a good shape.

Harvest

Harvest plums when they are fully ripe, for eating, and slightly underripe, for jam making.

Prunes

Choose a variety of plums that are suitable for drying. D'Agen or damson plums are good.

Wash fruit and lay them on a rack or a baking tray lined with baking paper. Don't overcrowd. Put them in the oven at 70°C for 8 hours. Keep checking to see when they are ready. Or place in a dehydrator for 10–12 hours. Store in an airtight container in the fridge.

P R U N E

Pomegranate

♈	**Plant** all year
◎	**Harvest** autumn
◷	**Growing time** 16–20 weeks
⚘	**Space between plants** 3 m
⊽	**Pots** yes
☀	**Aspect** sun
⇩	**Soil pH** 5.5–7.5
✳	**Frost tolerant** yes

Plant
Young trees can be bought in pots ready to plant. Dig a large hole and cultivate the soil with well-rotted manure (or an all-round fertiliser) and compost. Pull the tree from its pot and gently tickle the roots to loosen. Lower into the hole so the soil level matches the bottom of the tree. Backfill the hole with soil.

Nurture
Water young trees regularly especially in the first year when they're establishing roots. When established it doesn't require a lot of water but it is good to deep water your tree in the hottest part of summer. It is wise to compost around the base of the tree in spring and to add manure and top with mulch to keep the area from drying off.

Harvest
Fruit is ready in late autumn when it is the size of a large orange and is a lovely rosy colour.

Pomegranate molasses

Makes 2 preserving jars

Place pomegranate arils (fleshy seeds) in a blender and pulse just enough to create juice. Don't overblend so that the white bitter parts are totally blended in. Strain through a fine sieve or cloth. Wear gloves if you use cloth as you will need to squeeze it through and the juice stains.

Simmer in a small saucepan with the sugar and lemon for 1 hour or until it is syrupy and coats the back of a spoon. Adjustments to the sweetness or acidity can be made by adding more sugar or lemon. Pour into sterilised jars (see p. 190) and store in the fridge for up to 3 months.

Tip: The best way to remove the arils from the skins is to first roll the fruit under the palm of your hand along the bench with a bit of pressure. Then cut the pomegranate in half, hold it over a bowl with the cut side down and beat the skin with a wooden spoon until the arils drop out.

8 pomegranates (see note)
110 g (½ cup) granulated sugar
2 tbsp lemon juice

POMEGRANATE MOLASSES

Quince

♈	**Plant** all year
◎	**Harvest** autumn
☉	**Growing time until fruit** 2–4 years
❦	**Space between plants** 3 m
☖	**Pots** yes
☀	**Aspect** sun
⚓	**Soil pH** 5.5–7.5
❄	**Frost tolerant** yes

Varieties
Vranja – good for baking, poaching, preserves and jellies, light cropper
Meech's Prolific – heavy cropper
Rich's Dwarf – vigorous, rounded fruit

Plant
Young trees can be bought in pots ready to plant. Dig a large hole and cultivate the soil with well-rotted manure (or an all-round fertiliser) and compost. Pull the tree from its pot and gently tickle the roots to loosen. Lower into the hole so the soil level matches the bottom of the tree. Backfill the hole with soil.

Nurture
Water young trees regularly, especially in the first year when roots are developing. Once established it doesn't require a lot of water, but it is good to give your tree deep watering in the hottest part of summer. Compost around the base of the tree in spring, add manure and top with mulch to keep the area from drying out.

Harvest
Fruit is ready in autumn when it twists off easily. Pick fruit at the just-ripe stage for jelly and very ripe for quince paste. Don't allow the fruit to overripen on the tree, as it will become susceptible to fruit fly. The fruit can be stored in a cool place for 6 weeks.

Preserved poached quinces
Makes 6 medium preserving jars

Peel and core quinces and slice into 6 wedges per quince. Put quince in a large saucepan of water (the water should just cover them) with the sugar and vanilla pod. Bring to the boil and then gently simmer for 3–4 hours until the quinces are a deep rose colour. Transfer to sterilised jars and seal (see p. 190). The jars can be stored for up to a year.

10 quinces
800 g granulated sugar
1 vanilla pod, split and seeds scraped

QUINCES

NECTARINE

P O A C H

— D E H Y D R A T E

P E A C H

A P R I C O T

Varieties

APRICOTS
Bulida – dwarf variety, juicy, sweet
Divinity – early fruiter, popular

NECTARINES
Double Delight – sweet, mid-season
Fantasia – large, yellow flesh

PEACHES
Muir – resistant to curly leaf
Anzac – white fleshed, popular
Saturn – flat, white flesh

Stone fruit

♈	**Plant**	winter
◎	**Harvest**	summer, autumn
⏱	**Growing time**	16–20 weeks
⚘	**Space between plants**	3 m
⏶	**Pots**	possible
☀	**Aspect**	full sun
⇩	**Soil pH**	6.0–7.0
✳	**Frost tolerant**	yes

Plant

Stone fruit trees (apricots, peaches, nectarines) are self-pollinators so you can buy them singly.

Trees are best planted bare-rooted in winter when the tree is dormant. Young trees can be bought in pots ready to plant. Dig a large hole and cultivate the soil with well-rotted manure (or an all-round fertiliser) and compost. Pull the tree from its pot and gently tickle the roots to loosen. Lower into the hole so the soil level matches the bottom of the tree. Backfill the hole with soil. Hammer in two wooden stakes either side of the tree outside the root line. Use soft stretchy twine to tie the tree in place. This will protect it from being knocked. You can also wrap chicken wire or use agricultural plastic sleeves if you are in a rural area and animals are a risk.

Nurture

Fruit trees like to be watered deeply, so water weekly and for a long time so that the water goes deep into the soil. This will help with its root strength. Mulch around trees to retain moisture and fertilise with potash in spring. Peaches and nectarines are susceptible to curly leaf and need to be sprayed with copper fungicide just as the buds appear and before they open. The amount of fruit that sets will depend on the period when the tree is in blossom. If there are high winds or lots of rain this will spoil the blossom before pollination occurs. Some gardeners hand-pollinate with a paint brush, but if you have lots of bees they should do their job.

Trees will need netting to protect from birds. Always use sterilised tools and prune the tree after harvest when it is still in leaf. This reduces the risk of disease. Remove one-third of the branch lengths and any crossover branches so that there is an openness to the tree.

Harvest

Pick fruit as it ripens. You can pick earlier and ripen inside in a sunny spot. This is a way to get to them before the birds.

POACHED PEACHES WITH
CARDAMOM & VANILLA

Poached peaches in vanilla syrup

For 10–12

Wash peaches. Put the sugar into a large saucepan with 1.5 litres (6 cups) of water. Add the cardamom and the whole vanilla pod and seeds. Boil until the sugar has dissolved. Add the peaches to the pan and return to the boil. Poach gently for 15 minutes. Use a slotted spoon to remove the fruit and continue to cook the syrup until it thickens. Remove the skins from the peaches and return to the syrup. Serve warm or cooled with ice cream or cream. The peaches can also be bottled in the syrup into sterilised jars (see p. 190) and stored for up to a year.

1.5 kg peaches, skin and stones intact
660 g (3 cups) caster sugar
4 cardamom pods, bruised
1 vanilla pod, split and seeds scraped

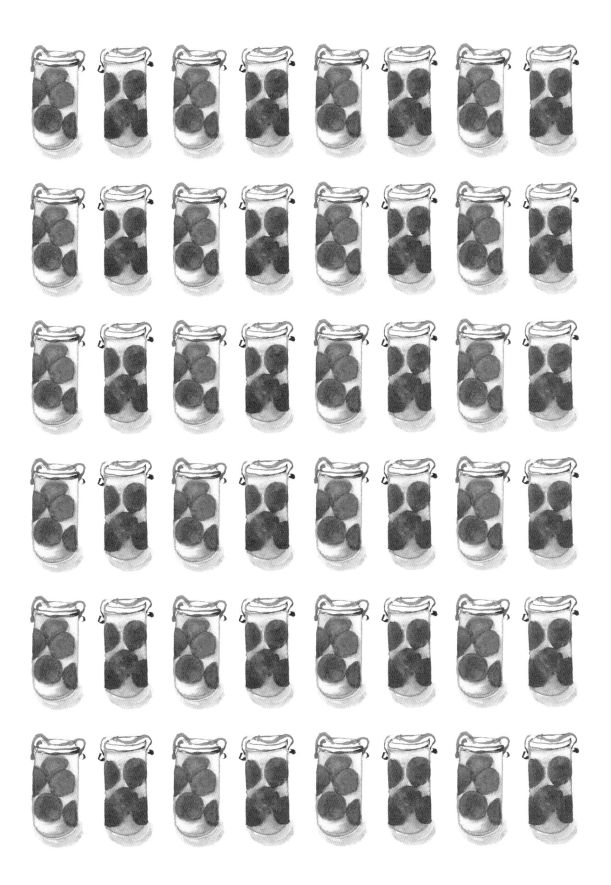

Chapter 06

All about your kitchen garden

Starting a vegetable garden can be somewhat daunting, but really it isn't difficult. I recommend planning ahead and finding the right spot in the garden. If you only have a balcony or rental property, start with a good selection of pots and think about their arrangement.

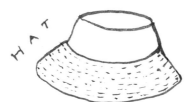

HAT

GLOVES

WATERING CAN

SHOVEL

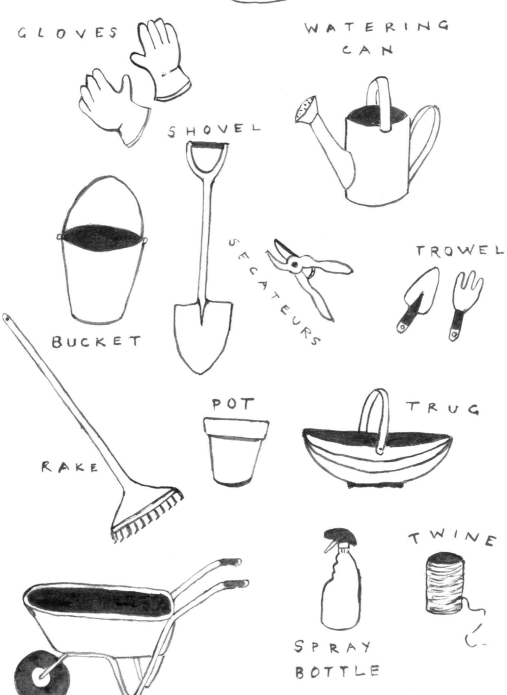

BUCKET

SECATEURS

TROWEL

RAKE

POT

TRUG

TWINE

SPRAY BOTTLE

WHEELBARROW

Where to start

Choose a spot that you can get water to easily and make sure it gets lots of sun. Almost all vegetables are sun lovers. Once you have followed the instructions in this chapter on how to build your soil and which plants go well next to other plants, you can get started. To begin with I would recommend buying in your seedlings, as seed germination takes time and diligence, and is something you can graduate to once you become an avid and confident gardener.

Bed placement

Vegetable beds need lots of sun: usually 4–5 hours a day. If you are choosing to build raised beds, they need to have space in between to move a wheelbarrow. It's good to have some beds in light shade to protect them from the harsh summer sun and a sheltered spot away from the prevailing winds. Proximity to a garden tap is also essential. Container gardens such as pots are useful to have close to the kitchen door for ease of picking, especially herbs.

Watering

It amuses me (now that I know better) how inefficiently I used to water my garden: just standing there wiggling the hose over the plants and flipping over to another bed and doing the same thing just ain't going to cut it. Deep, long watering less often is much more beneficial to most plants as it encourages the roots to go deep, and therefore they become less vulnerable to heat stress. The hardier the plant, the less likely it is susceptible to diseases and pests.

To water really well, you need to set up a watering system and put it on a timer system. Then, by the time you get up in the morning, all your garden beds will have been watered. Watering systems have an array of nozzles to meet the demands of various plants: from light spray to heavier flow, while some work best with a drip system. Controlled and regular watering seems to create a healthier vegetable garden. I usually set my timer to water for 30 minutes 2–3 times a week at the height of summer, less in the spring and autumn.

Watering is best done either in the evening or in the morning, and never in the middle of the day if it's extremely hot. Although if you see a distressed plant you can water low at the roots.

If you still prefer to hand-water, it's a good idea to dig down and see how effectively you have watered. It takes a considerable time before you get the whole bed deeply watered. If you stick your finger into the soil it should feel wet right to the end of your finger.

Soil

I can't emphasise how important attention to soil is. All garden beds need a regular topping up of humus (organic matter) and nutrients. Maintaining soil condition is the hard slog of the garden jobs, but the one that will bring you the best results. Start by knowing your soil.

Soil type testing

Do you have clay, sandy or loamy soil? Take a handful of soil from your intended vegetable patch and dampen it with a spray bottle of water. Squeeze the soil in your hand to create a sausage shape. The results will be one of the three here:

CLAY SOIL will hold shape and, when poked with your finger, will remain solid.

Clay soil is usually rich in nutrients, but doesn't allow the water to drain freely, so it has a tendency to become either waterlogged or too compacted. It is referred to as heavy soil. It is particularly difficult to grow root vegetables in heavy soil, so it is better for brassicas, such as broccoli and cabbages.

The fix: Sprinkle unplanted beds with gypsum (follow application guidelines on the packaging) and dig through. Add a thick layer of compost (see opposite page) mixed through with rotted-down manure or fertiliser pellets. A thick layer of mulch, such as pea straw, should then be added on top to keep the soil from drying out. Then leave it for a couple of weeks before planting. It will become a happy home for beneficial insects and worms who will happily work your soil for you.

SANDY SOIL will be difficult to mould into a sausage shape and will remain in a crumbly state.

Sandy soils have large particles with spaces in between called pore spaces that hold the oxygen needed by plants; however, sandy soils tend to be low in nutrients. It is referred to as light soil. This type of soil is easy to cultivate, but water drains away too quickly, causing your garden beds to be dry. It is better for root vegetables.

The fix: Compost and rotted-down manure (or fertiliser pellets) should be worked into the soil. The compost will improve the structure and the manure will add nutrients to your soil. Mulch the top to retain moisture.

LOAMY SOIL will hold the sausage shape, but when poked it will crumble. If you have loamy soil, it is perfect for growing vegetables.

CLAY

SANDY

LOAMY

Soil pH testing

This is another important factor in growing your vegetables. You can feel like a chemistry nerd and buy an inexpensive testing kit from your gardening store. Getting the right pH in your soil to match your crop will see your vegetables thrive.

A pH of 7 is considered neutral, 14 is extremely alkaline and 0 is extremely acid. Ideally, a pH of 5.5–7.5 is a healthy soil for most vegetables. To raise the pH add lime, and to lower it add sulphur, according to the instructions on the packet. This is usually a temporary fix so it's a good idea to test before planting your crops each season.

If you get your soil right then you are well on your way to winning the prize at the local agricultural show. Just about all types of soil can be rectified with a bit of attention before you plant. There is something very pleasing in turning over a sod of soil and seeing that it is rich, moist, loamy and alive with garden worms.

Layering of compost, manure and mulch needs to be repeated before spring, summer and autumn planting. You can get away with less than that, but if you want that show prize, just do it!

Compost

There are entire books on how to compost and to some it is as important as stacking the dishwasher correctly. I'm a bit haphazard with both. Basically, for a good compost, you need a combination of green matter and brown matter. These make up the carbon and nitrogen mix which carries all the microorganisms that produce compost. When compost is used it improves the structure of the soil and also adds nutrients. It acts as an 'organic sponge' reservoir and therefore retains the moisture in the soil. It can be used as a soil additive, fertiliser and mulch, and without it you won't have much luck growing anything!

It is possible to buy compost in the form of mushroom compost or similar from garden suppliers, but every household disposes of enormous amounts of vegetable waste, so why not use it? It's free.

It's worth concentrating on how to make really good compost.

Compost bins come in all shapes and sizes and where you live will determine what kind of bin

you can manage. If you are in an apartment it might be better to invest in a worm farm as they don't need much space. If you have a good-sized garden you might like to build a compost enclosure out of wood. Most bins are approximately a metre or so square with slatted sides for ventilation. Large garden centres have plastic bins with a lid as another option. We have three wooden compartments in a row on rotation, which works well for us.

The ingredients for a good compost:

GREEN MATTER (Nitrogen)
Grass clippings
Manure (chicken, cow, sheep, horse)
Green prunings
Kitchen fruit and vegetable scraps (not citrus, garlic or onions, as worms aren't into them)
Old flowers
Weeds
Tea leaves and coffee grounds
Fresh leaves
Eggshells
Vegetable oils

BROWN MATTER (Carbon)
Non-coated cardboard
Paper
Untreated wood chips
Dry leaves
Sawdust
Dry grass clippings
Straw
Ash

The 'lasagne method' uses green and brown matter applied in distinct, flat layers, sometimes with soil added between the layers. This is a simple and practical method.

A compost heap needs to be kept moist by regular watering and it is essential to keep it aerated by turning it with a pitchfork or compost aerator tool. If your compost is smelly, you will need to add more brown matter; if it is too dry it is lacking green matter.

The compost heap will warm up as the organisms do their thing. A core temperature of 60°C should be enough to destroy weed seeds. It takes a couple of months to break down into usable compost, so it is good to have a few compartments at varying stages of breaking down.

Worm farms

Worm farms are particularly good in city gardens where space is an issue, and because a happy worm farm is odourless, they can even be housed inside. Worms convert organic waste into nutrient-rich fertiliser. The worms' manure, or 'castings', is a source of vital plant nutrients, minerals and microorganisms and can be steeped and diluted to make worm tea – a great liquid fertiliser for your garden.

Worms and worm farm kits can be purchased from garden suppliers and online. You can, however, make your own and there is a lot of information available on the internet on how to do that.

When feeding the worm farm, it is best to keep the scraps cut up into small pieces, even blending the scraps if you can. Feed in scraps a couple of times a week.

The worm farm should never smell bad if it is being looked after correctly. If it does smell, add shredded cardboard and create more air holes and allow the farm to settle before adding more green waste. The worm farm should be kept out of the sun and under cover.

What to feed worms:

Vegetables
Fruit
Eggshells
Coffee grounds
Unprinted cardboard
Dead flowers and cuttings

What not to feed worms:

Meat
Dairy
Citrus
Onions
Fats or oils

Fertiliser

Plants in their natural habitat usually have everything they need to survive or even thrive. Drawing from their natural environment, they work within their own ecosystem. Their leaves fall and naturally decompose, putting the right nutrients back into the soil to feed the microorganisms. They often rely on other flora with which they cohabit for shade or protection from the wind. In home gardens we tend to clear away the plant debris or harvest it instead of allowing it to compost back into the surrounding soil. This disrupts the plant's natural life cycle and therefore we need to add organic matter and fertilisers to help our plants grow.

Adding compost and mulch is a great pathway to healthy plants; however, more nutrients are often needed. For this, you need to add fertiliser. Fertiliser comes in either a natural or synthetic form.

Garden centres sell fertiliser in the form of granules and liquid. This is convenient, especially for gardeners in the city, where sacks of manure with honesty boxes are few and far between. I do, however, have a preference for the more organic fertiliser as it properly replenishes the soil.

You may also need to test your soil (with a soil testing kit from your local garden centre) to see what type of nutrients you need to apply. See soil testing (p. 159) for help with this.

The three main nutrients that plants need are:

NITROGEN – this stimulates plant growth above the soil, especially leaf growth.

PHOSPHORUS – this is particularly good for root growth and is beneficial to young seedlings.

POTASSIUM (POTASH) – this is to promote all-round plant health and help with disease resistance.

Liquid fertiliser

There are organic or inorganic liquid fertilisers, and both are effective and have their benefits. Liquid fertiliser is very effective in getting nutrients to the plant quickly. It is absorbed within 24 hours of its application, directly into the plant's foliage and root system. It should be applied regularly in the summer months, as much as once a week for plants like tomatoes. Liquid feeding also adds to the plant's resilience during the hottest and coldest times of the year.

Homemade liquid fertiliser teas are easy to make and cost virtually nothing. Worm tea from your own worm farm is fantastic. There are other methods that also work well, such as a couple of spadefuls of manure inside an old pillowcase, tied and submerged in a big bucket of water: after a couple of days, it is good to go. This can also be done with weeds and lawn clippings. Nettle tea is a particularly good liquid fertiliser. With gloves on, shove nettles into a pair of pantyhose (which is a much better use than wearing them) and dangle them in a giant bucket of water for a week or so. It is important to dilute the tea concentrate to 1:10 ratio before using. Simply mix into a watering can and apply.

Manure

Choosing your manure really depends on what is available to you. They all work; a mix is even better. The important thing to remember is that no fresh manure should be added to soil, not unless you have time for it to decompose from its raw state before planting. This is usually a 2–3 week process. If your beds have seedlings already on the go you can mix the manure with compost and leave it in a pile until the decomposing has happened, then apply. The manure needs to be at an almost dry state when added in the presence of plants. Sometimes it comes bagged and already dry, often gathered from under a wool shed or dry from the paddocks. Chicken manure can be bought in pellet form from garden centres for easy and immediate use. Apply to garden beds at the beginning of spring and again in autumn.

Chicken – high in nitrogen with no seeds from weeds. Needs to be well rotted down as it will burn plants in its raw form. This can be bought in dry pellets.

Cow – good all-rounder, but can contain weed seeds.

Horse – can have traces of undigested herbicides that can harm plants. Needs to be rotted down.

Sheep – high in nitrogen and phosphorus, easy to distribute.

Mulch

Once I discovered mulch my garden beds went from being ho-hum to FABULOUS! Mulching also cuts out a lot of time spent weeding. I would water and water and water (there are tricks to watering, too) and still my vegetables would be sagging and wilting in constantly dry beds. I now shudder when I see garden beds without a loving protective blanket of mulch. On top of your mix of compost it is beneficial to add a thick layer of mulch. This helps to retain the moisture and acts as a weed mat, as well as insulating your beds from the harsh elements.

Good mulch comes in the form of pea straw, lucerne, straw, sugarcane shreddings, woodchips, bark, dry grass clippings (unsprayed), black plastic or geotextiles and untreated cardboard.

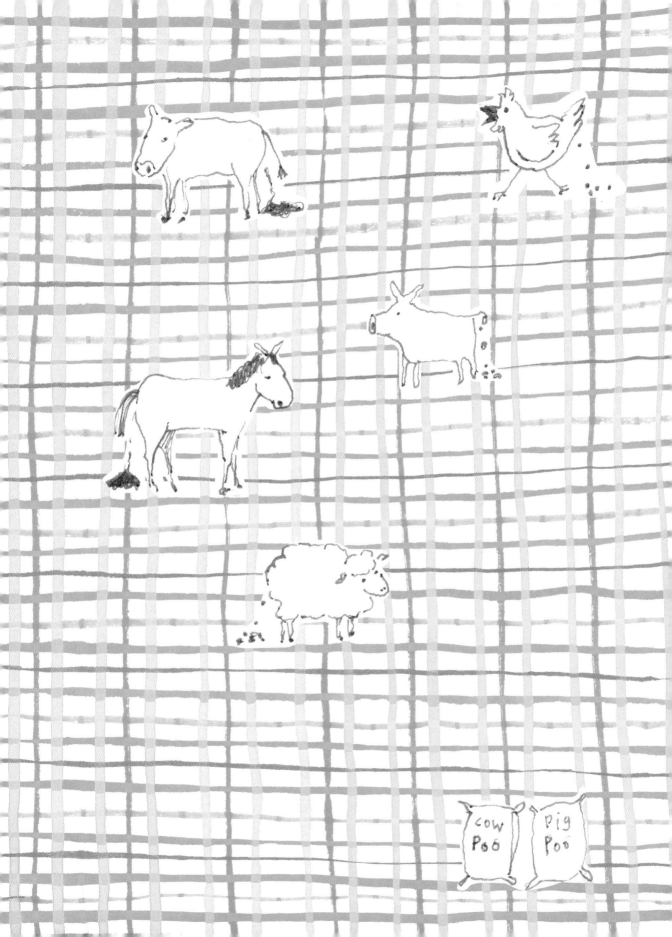

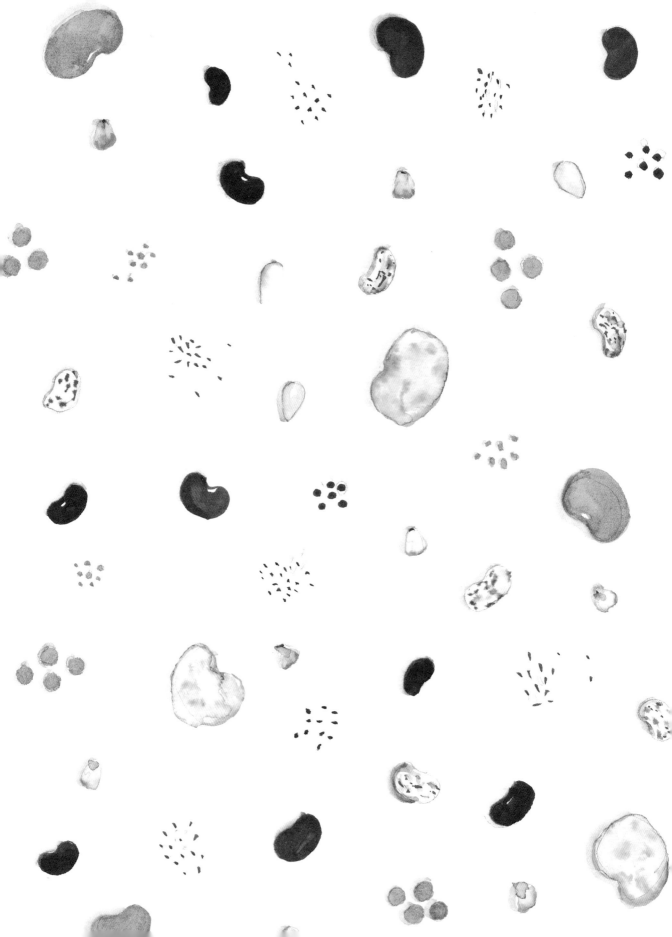

Seeds to seedlings

Germinating seeds can be fun and can satisfy all your nurturing needs in one. Like any newborn they require a lot of attention. They need a comfy warm bed, regular feeding and gentle watering, even singing and humming works. There are days of anticipation waiting for your little darlings to spring to life in the most delicate and fragile way. The love is there right from the beginning.

The key to success in the nursery is to plant more than you need. There isn't a 100 per cent success rate, so if you are dropping seeds into planting pods, place two in each pod and when they sprout eliminate the weaker one by pinching it out (I know, brutal).

Source your seeds from the most reputable plant suppliers. Some specialise in heirloom varieties, which I recommend. This means they are open-pollinated and therefore the seeds you collect from these plants will replicate the parent plant. They also tend to be a better-quality seed.

There are three main types of seeds in the vegetable garden:

seeds in pods – such as peas and beans

plants with small dry seeds – such as celery, parsley and basil

seeds in fleshy fruits – such as tomatoes

Collecting seeds

I would only recommend saving seeds from the following vegetables:

Tomatoes
Capsicums
Peas and beans
Parsley
Basil
Green onions

Other seeds of vegetables tend to throw a different and less robust plant than their mother plant.

Parsley
seeds
8·9·21

SEEDS IN PODS Allow the pods to dry and brown on the plant. Pick and remove the dry pods and lay them on a tray indoors to dry further. After a couple of weeks, shell and store the seeds in paper bags. Remember to date and label. The remaining pods can be thrown onto your compost heap.

SMALL SEEDS Cut flower heads that have dried off on the plant and shake the seeds into paper bags, label and store.

SEEDS FROM FLESHY PLANTS Allow the vegetable to fully ripen on the plant. Scoop out seeds and pulp and put them into a jar of water for a few days until the seeds have dropped to the bottom and the pulp remains at the top. You might have to give them a swirl every now and then. Drain and pour seeds onto a paper towel to dry. When dry they can be stored in a labelled paper bag.

Germinating your seeds

The important thing to remember when germinating seeds is that they need to be undercover in a greenhouse or on a windowsill. They need warmth, protection from winds and constant moisture. You can buy mini greenhouses that work well. The general rule of thumb is that the seed should be buried to twice the depth of the seed size.

You will need a good quality seedling mix that is loose in structure. A mix of fine compost and soil is okay. Or you can buy it ready-made, which is probably best.

Choose a container to start the seedlings in. This can be store bought or you can use toilet rolls, egg cartons or small plastic tubs with holes at the bottom. You can buy clever seedling pods that can go in the ground with the seedling so the roots aren't disturbed.

After a couple of weeks prick out the strong seedlings and transfer into bigger pots. When the seedling is good and strong and there is no risk of frost damage you can plant them in your garden beds.

TO PLANT SEEDS:

- fill the container with soil mixture and pack down very lightly

- gently water

- sprinkle in seeds: bury to twice the depth of the seed size or follow instructions on the packet

- mulch with vermiculite grains to stop drying out

- keep them from drying out by spraying them with water daily

- keep them on a windowsill, greenhouse or mini seedling greenhouse tray

Growing in pots

There are many vegetables that are suitable for growing in pots and containers. Some plants, such as zucchini, which grows to a metre across, should have their own container, while others can share. It's important to know how big your plant will grow and to choose a pot to accommodate it. It is wise to have a collection of pots at the back door with herbs or salad leaves so that they are handy when cooking.

It's up to you what your pot may be. There are some crazy and quirky ones made from old watering cans, wheelbarrows and even tyres if that pleases you. I prefer regular pots in different sizes and heights mixed in with flowering annuals. The most important thing to remember is to keep up the watering and the liquid fertiliser feeds. A good-quality potting mix is also essential with mesh or stones at the bottom of the pot for good drainage.

Potatoes can be grown in special potato bags in canvas with a flap to access the potatoes. This is a novel and convenient way to grow them. Another benefit: the potting mix doesn't get compacted and therefore the potatoes are easy to harvest.

Cherry tomatoes are fabulous in pots alongside basil and salad greens. I've seen pumpkins and beans growing on balconies in Italy, twisting through the railings, which act as a perfect trellis.

Raised beds are very popular and a good way of growing vegetables in containers. Keep in mind when choosing your raised beds that if you make them very deep they take rather a lot of filling. I ran into this problem and decided to half fill them with straw bales and then my soil and compost. As the soil compresses you will need to keep building up the layers with more compost and mulch.

If you decide to build your own raised garden beds, it is important that you choose untreated wood as treated wood leaches toxins into the soil and consequently into your vegetables. If building them isn't your thing, there are all sorts of store-bought options available at garden centres.

Container gardens

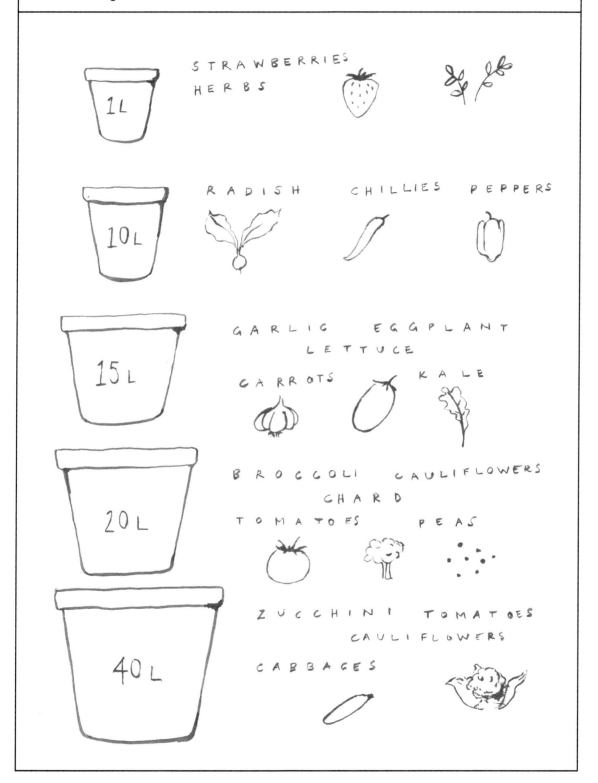

1 L — STRAWBERRIES HERBS

10 L — RADISH CHILLIES PEPPERS

15 L — GARLIC EGGPLANT LETTUCE CARROTS KALE

20 L — BROCCOLI CAULIFLOWERS CHARD TOMATOES PEAS

40 L — ZUCCHINI TOMATOES CAULIFLOWERS CABBAGES

Companion planting

Companion planting is the planting of crops in proximity to each other for beneficial reasons. This can be for pest control, pollination, maximising space, creating habitat for beneficial insects and crop productivity.

Permaculturists believe in scattered planting styles rather than large groups or rows that pests are more likely to home in on. Companion planting is a clever way of promoting plant health and is a way to work naturally within our environment without the overuse of pesticides and chemicals. Each of the plants covered in this book has a list of suggested companion plants.

Growing flowers among your vegetables will encourage bees and other insects and therefore your vegetables are more likely to be pollinated. Yellow and orange flowers in particular are bug attractors. Taller plants can provide shelter for plants that need protection or can be a structure for climbing plants to grow up. Some plants are good companions because their roots grow to different depths so they then don't compete for water or nutrients. Legumes (such as peas and beans) can promote the growth of nearby plants with their nitrogen-fixing ability.

Companion planting is a good way to trick those pesky bugs. Herbs can mask the scent of other plants and deter infestations. Brightly coloured flowers also attract bugs away from your precious veggies. (See planting charts on p. 194.)

HERBS THAT HELP:

Chives next to carrots (carrot fly), apples, berries, peas, tomatoes (aphids)

Lavender next to brassicas (lots of different pests)

Borage next to most vegetables (for most pests)

Nasturtiums next to beans (aphids), cucumber (cucumber beetles), apples, potatoes, pumpkins, radishes, squash

Basil next to tomatoes (white fly), eggplant, lettuce, capsicums

Rosemary next to cabbages and other brassicas (cabbage moths), peas, beans (weevil and bean beetles)

Sage next to brassicas (cabbage moths)

Peppermint next to most plants (slugs)

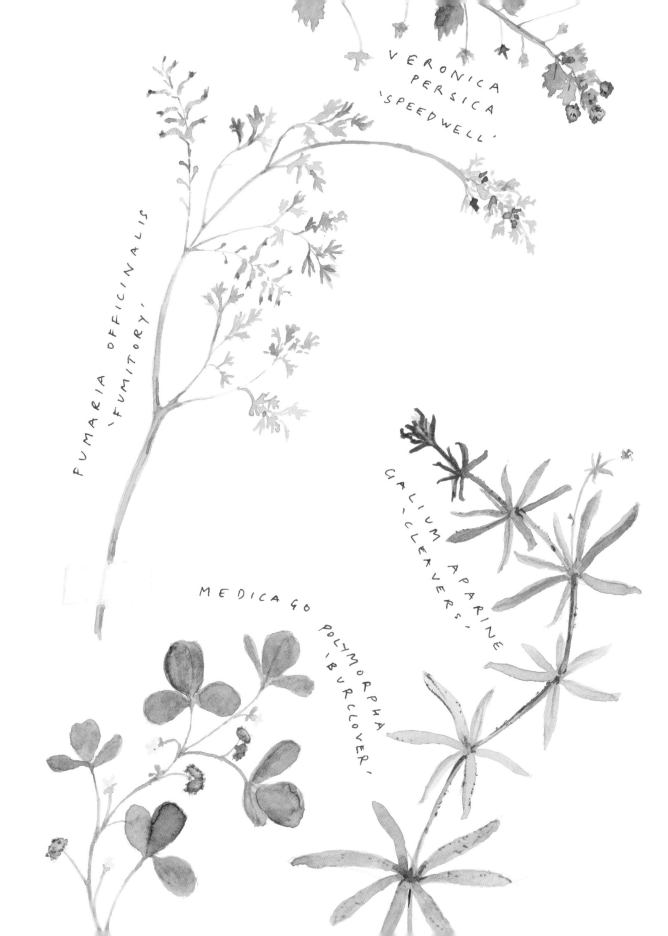

VERONICA
PERSICA
'SPEEDWELL'

FUMARIA OFFICINALIS
'FUMITORY'.

GALIUM APARINE
'CLEAVERS'.

MEDICAGO POLYMORPHA
'BURCLOVER'.

Weeds

There are some weeds that are definitely welcome in my garden. I particularly love nettles and dandelions. Both take up a firm spot in my kitchen pantry. There are many others I have tried, but I think I would only embrace them if I were to become lost and starving while bushwalking (unlikely); however, it is good to have some knowledge of what's edible when weeds jostle for space amongst the vegetable and flower beds.

Killing weeds

My sister-in-law, who has a lovely perennial garden, says she loves weeding. Especially when she is cross. By the time she has ploughed her way through a couple of decent-sized beds she is serene as can be. I'm trying to adopt this attitude: I particularly hate weeding, it's about as much fun as ironing. But, I have discovered some entertaining methods to do the deed.

THE FIRE WAND METHOD: Using heat from a flame weeder to kill weeds is best suited to garden paths. The residual heat makes it hard to home in on specific areas in a garden bed. In fact, my neighbour scorched an entire hedge! So on driveways and paths it is good, just keep away from the hedge. Check to see if there are any fire restrictions on your day of use.

CONCOCTIONS: I did read that vodka was good but seriously who would do that? What a Bloody Mary waste that would be! This one works: mix 2 litres of household-strength vinegar with half a cup of salt and a tablespoon of dishwashing liquid until completely dissolved. Pour into a spray bottle and you are good to go. Spray directly onto the weeds, being careful to avoid your plants.

BOILING WATER: This also works, but it is time consuming waiting for the kettle to boil and each weed needs a good cupful to die. If you have a small garden this method might appeal.

MULCH: Now you're talking! Mulching is essential to a successful vegetable garden anyway, so this method is a no-brainer. Mulch in the form of straw, woodchips, bark, cardboard or black plastic sheeting are all brilliant and effective ways of keeping out the weeds. Black plastic or cardboard is a great way to kill off weeds as the first step in preparing a new garden bed. Just lay it out over the desired area and leave it for a couple of weeks.

RIP THEM OUT BY THE ROOTS: adopt my sister-in-law's attitude and pull out all of life's woes with every weed... Ahh, that's better!

Eating weeds

Before you launch into eating a bowl of weeds, it is necessary to do a quick web search to check which ones are safe to eat. Some are toxic. It should also be noted that many weeds on the side of the road and footpath are sprayed with pesticides. Only pick your weeds from a place where you are certain that they haven't been sprayed.

Stinging nettles

Harvest young nettles (throw the seed heads back into your garden for more to grow) and *always* use gloves. Nettles are highly nutritious, full of antioxidants and have anti-inflammatory properties.

Nettle soup

For 6

Wash the nettles and pat dry with paper towel.

In a large saucepan, melt the butter and oil, then add the onion, celery, leek and nettles and sauté until soft. Pour in the stock and bring to the boil. Add the potato and simmer for 20 minutes.

Blitz in a food processor or blender and add cream to taste. Season with salt and pepper.

Big bunch of nettles, trimmed of seeds
50 g butter
Splash of oil
1 brown onion, coarsely chopped.
2 celery stalks, chopped
1 leek, washed and sliced
1 litre vegetable or chicken stock
1 potato, peeled and diced
Cream, to serve
Salt and pepper

Nettle risotto

For 4

Bring a saucepan of water to the boil. Meanwhile, wash the nettles and pat dry with paper towel. Plunge into boiling water to blanch, then drain and finely chop the nettles.

Use a heavy, deep-sided frying pan. Melt 50 g of the butter with a little oil, add the onion and sauté till translucent. Add the rice and stir to coat until glossy. Add wine and stir gently until all the liquid is taken up in the rice.

Add the hot stock a ladleful at a time, stirring constantly. Go gently and make sure each ladle of stock is absorbed before adding the next one. After about 10 minutes, add the nettles and continue to add ladles of stock until the rice is al dente. Stir in the remaining butter and the parmesan. Remove from the heat, cover with a clean tea towel and set aside to rest for 5 minutes before serving.

Big bunch of nettles, trimmed of seeds
125 g butter
splash of oil
1 onion, finely chopped
400 g arborio rice
125 ml (½ cup) dry white wine
2 litres chicken or vegetable stock, kept hot on the stove
100 g parmesan cheese, grated or crumbled

Nettle pesto

Using a mortar and pestle, pound a bunch of washed and dried nettle leaves together with a handful of pine nuts, a good pinch of flaky salt and a garlic clove until a paste forms. Transfer to a jar and pour in some good quality olive oil to your desired consistency. Makes one 300 ml jar.

Dandelions

Dandelions usually grow in swathes so keep your eyes peeled for a lovely meadow full. Only pick flowers that are away from car emissions and are not from areas that council might have sprayed with herbicides.

Dandelion jelly

Makes 4 small preserving jars

This is like sunshine in a jar. Luscious yellow jelly that tastes like floral honey.

3 cups of dandelion flower heads, washed

1 litre (4 cups) boiling water

Juice of ½ a lemon

1 packet of jam pectin (28.5 g)

4 cups sugar

Pull the petals from the flower heads and discard the green parts. You should have about 2 packed cups of petals. Put them in a heatproof bowl and pour the boiling water over. Cover and set aside to steep for at least 3 hours, or up to 24 hours.

Strain the water into a large saucepan, add lemon juice and jam pectin and bring to the boil. Add the sugar and bring back to the boil for a couple of minutes. Use the jam testing method on p. 190 to check if your jelly is ready.

Pour into heated sterilised preserving jars (see p. 190), seal with the lid and place them in a canning bath (such as a large saucepan). Cover with water and bring to the boil for 15 minutes. Carefully remove from the bath and place the jars on a wooden chopping board to cool.

Store in the refrigerator for up to 6 months.

VIOLET

VIOLA

DIANTHUS

NASTURTIUM

CORNFLOWER

Edible flowers

I'm not a huge fan of smothering cakes in edible flowers; however, I do think a very light scattering of some dried petals can look good, or if the flowers are added to create a floral note to a dish (rather than just for decoration) it works. I particularly like the very old-fashioned method of crystallising flowers. Frosted violets and pansies can give a delicate and pretty addition to a creamy lemony frosting. Tiny herb flowers, especially thyme and rosemary flowers, are lovely on cakes with syrup.

Borage – pretty blue star-shaped flowers that taste like cucumber

Chamomile – mild apple notes

Chive flowers – pretty delicate purple flowers that have a chive flavour so best for savoury dishes

Dianthus, cornflower – use flower petals only, has a clove-like taste

Elderflower – floral vanilla notes

Lavender – kind of citrus/floral flavour

Marigold, calendula – use the orange–yellow petals only; they taste slightly sweet but also a little salty

Nasturtium – both the flower and leaves are edible; the leaves have a peppery taste and the flowers a sweeter nectar taste

Rose petals – use fresh or dried on cakes or puddings

Violet and viola – bake onto biscuits or use fresh on cakes or salads as they are sweet and floral

Nasturtium leaves and flowers are popular in salads and add a nice peppery flavour (but don't overdo it). Recently a lovely friend of mine reminisced about a delicious sandwich his grandmother used to make. He remembers fresh white bread simply with butter and nasturtium leaves. This is the kind of grandmother I love!

It's important to say that many flowers are toxic and therefore should never be added to the top of cakes or salads. Caution also must be taken to avoid flowers that have been sprayed with insecticide, fungicide and herbicide.

NASTURTIUM LEAF SANDWICH

C R Y S T A L L I S E D

V I O L E T S

Crystallised violets

In a small bowl, combine 1 egg white with a few drops of water and whisk lightly until the white just shows a few bubbles. Put some caster sugar in a shallow dish. If you just have granulated sugar, put the sugar (½ cup at a time) into a blender and whiz until the sugar is broken into smaller crystals.

Holding a flower or petal in one hand, dip a small paint brush into the egg white with the other and gently paint the flower. Cover the flower or petal completely but not too generously.

Holding the flower or petal over the sugar dish, gently sprinkle sugar evenly all over on all sides. Turn the flower so excess sugar falls off. It is not necessary to shake it. Place the violet on waxed paper to dry. Continue with the rest of the flowers.

Let the flowers dry completely; they should be free of moisture. If you have a dehydrator, dry them for several hours on a low heat. You can place the candied flowers in an oven set at the lowest temperature (50–90°C) with the door ajar for a few hours.

Store the dried, candied flowers in airtight containers until ready to use. They will keep for as long as a year.

Herbs

Herbs are one of the most useful and money-saving additions to the kitchen garden. How often is there a sagging bunch of herbs in the fridge? Usually only a day or so after purchase. Growing herbs allows you to pick as much as you need, as you require it. Herbs can be used in almost all dishes from salads to cakes. They are also spectacular in drinks and teas. I like to mix herbs in with flowers when putting together a posy from the garden: the smell is heavenly.

Perennial herbs

Chamomile – used for tea

Chives – soups, salads, vegetables

Lemon balm – good on fruit salad and tea

Lemon verbena – nice in tea

Lovage – good in casseroles, soups, salads and also celery like

Mint – drinks, fruit

Oregano – good in tomato dishes, good to dehydrate

Rosemary – potatoes, poultry, vegetables

Sage – poultry, pork, soups

Sweet marjoram – poultry, soups, potatoes

Tarragon – sauces, salads

Thyme – great with vegetables and in syrups for cakes

Perennial herbs are easy to grow and they are like the gift that keeps on giving. Every spring they will reappear. Here are some popular and useful ones to grow.

mint

lemon verbena

chamomile

lemon balm

Annual herbs

Basil – tomatoes, soups, salads

Chervil – salads

Coriander – Asian cuisine

Dill – seafood, salads

Fennel leaves – salads, seafood

Parsley – most useful herb in many dishes

Annual herbs need to be resown each year; however, if you leave your herbs to the point of going to seed they will often self-seed in the same spot.

Herbal tea

My friend Caroline Parker (The Cottage Herbalist) is the queen of tea. This is her Garden Tea.

Pick a small handful of nettles, plantain weed, chickweed, thyme, sage, calendula, mint, catnip, sorrel, lavender leaves and dandelion petals.

Place all of the herbs in a large teapot and pour in boiling water. Allow to brew for a few minutes and pour into your favourite cup.

Sip with both hands snugly wrapped around your cup.

HERBAL TEA

Vegetable scrap garden

It's possible and surprising to regrow vegetables from the scraps. Some vegetable scraps can be re-used to grow the foliage part of the plant, which is useful for salads and stir-fries, and some can be rebooted and planted out to become full plants again.

The most important thing to do is to keep the water fresh.

Vegetables suitable for re-use:

Onions, leeks, green onions – the root base that has been sliced off can be placed in a shallow dish of water and when regrowth appears they can be planted out.

Celery – this is the hero in the scrap regrowing comp. Simply slice from the base leaving stems about 5cm long. Submerge the base in water and wait a week or so for growth. You can harvest leaves from your windowsill or you can plant it out again for a full plant.

Fennel – use the same method as celery.

Root vegetables (carrots, swedes, parsnips, beetroot) – slice the root off near the foliage leaving a couple of centimetres. Stand it in a tray with water. The foliage can be used in salads or stir-fries. The root can be replanted in the garden.

Lettuce, cabbage – when harvesting from the vegetable garden, slice from the base and leave the roots to regrow.

Herbs – put 10 cm long stems in a glass of water, being careful to have any leaves well above the waterline. Once roots regrow, plant out into your vegetable bed.

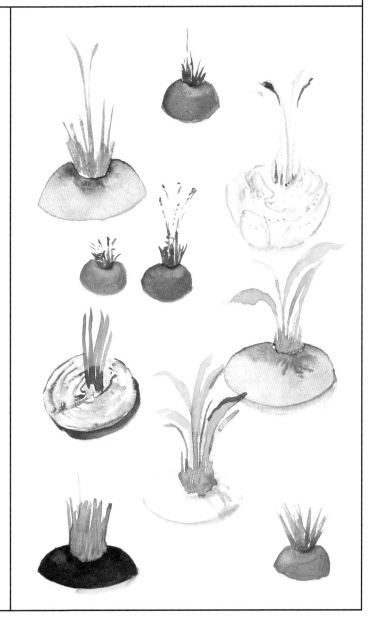

Pests and diseases

It can be very disheartening when your vegetable garden has succumbed to pests or disease. With careful attention to creating healthy plants, it is possible to reduce your chances of being infested using the following organic methods and clever techniques.

Crop rotation

As well as rejuvenating soils in some instances, crop rotation is a brilliant way of deterring pests and diseases. I spent years ignoring crop rotation rules until I started having trouble with my tomatoes and decided to take it seriously. Fungus and spores live on in the soil, so moving crops along to a different bed decreases the chances of the diseases taking hold in the same plant the following year. Crop rotation also allows plants to benefit from the previous crop's nutrients. In the case of legumes, they help replenish nitrogen by collecting available nitrogen from the atmosphere and storing it in nodules on their root structure; this is then left in the soil to the benefit of the next crop. Legumes always follow the nitrogen hungry brassicas for that reason. Rotation reduces any build-up of disease in the soil, and keeps pests guessing where their favourite plants are.

There are four main groups of vegetables that are good on rotation: legumes, brassicas, alliums and solanums. These groups are closely related and therefore share the same growing conditions and attract the same pests and diseases. The list below shows the ideal order of rotation.

LEGUMES – broad beans, dwarf beans, peas, runner beans

SOLANUMS – potatoes, tomatoes

ALLIUMS – garlic, leeks, onions, green onions

BRASSICAS – broccoli, cabbage, kale, kohlrabi, bok choy, radishes, swedes, turnips

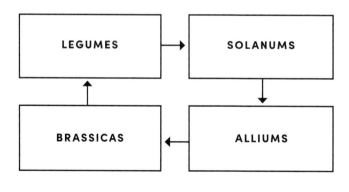

Common garden pests

curl grub

Cabbage moth larvae

slugs

Cucumber beetle

harlequin beetles

lacewing moths

earwigs

aphids

potato moth

birds

root eelworm

Green vegetable beetle

Netting

Choosing the right kind of net is important. Cabbage moths are clever at squeezing through large-weave nets, and once inside they are trapped and do extra damage. It is worth putting in a bit of time creating a frame that will hold the nets above your plants.

Make sure the sides are securely fixed with no holes. It is good, however, that other beneficial bugs can still slide though to help pollinate. Always check nets for birds or animals that might get trapped.

cabbage moth

Snail traps or deterrents

Please don't use snail pellets; they can be deadly for pets and wildlife. An easy way to deter snails is to sink paper cups into the soil and half fill them with beer. The snail will slide in and drown: sorry, snails! Another method is to sprinkle coffee grounds or crushed eggshells around your seedlings, a method that not only deters snails but improves the soil.

snail

Homemade remedies

It is surprising how efficient homemade remedies are. They probably don't keep as well as store-bought products, but they are cheaper and there is something nice about mixing up these concoctions. They are generally safe to use and a great way to involve children in making them and applying them.

Neem oil spray

Makes 500 ml spray bottle

Put the ingredients in the spray bottle and fill the bottle with water. Shake to combine.

Neem oil is good as an insecticide and a fungicide. Spray directly onto the leaves of the plants weekly until the problem is solved.

1 tsp organic cold-pressed neem oil
1 tsp liquid castile soap
1 tsp peppermint essential oil

Bug deterrent spray

Makes 500 ml spray bottle

Put the ingredients in the spray bottle and fill the bottle with water. Shake to combine. Spray directly onto the leaves of the plants weekly to deter aphids, earwigs, mealybugs and whitefly.

½ tsp bicarb soda
1 tsp liquid castile soap

Chive spray

Makes 500 ml spray bottle

Put the chives and flowers in a heatproof bowl and pour the boiling water over. Cover and set aside to cool completely. Strain and pour into the spray bottle. Add the soap and shake to combine.

Use chive spray as an antifungal to treat powdery mildew. Spray directly onto the leaves of affected plants, usually once a week until the problem is solved.

1 cup chives and chive flowers
500 ml (2 cups) boiling water
1 tsp liquid castile soap

Keeping bees and chickens

Animals and insects play a major role in the vegetable garden. I have both bees and chickens and they fill me with joy every time I'm out in the garden. Having your own honey and eggs along with your own vegetables is halfway to not having to visit the supermarket.

Chickens

We happened to inherit one of the country's finest chicken coops. Built by the previous owners, it is certainly the main feature of our garden. It was designed so that the chickens had a free run of the orchard. At some stage we rearranged the garden, making some areas less restricted and therefore the chickens found a new and vast garden to explore. They moved around in their happy way, kind of gossiping in a girly pack, fossicking and pecking and scuffing about. If we sat outside and had a cup of tea we were always joined by the chickens alongside our three-legged Staffy dog, Digby. I adored having the chickens roaming the whole garden, almost nothing pleased me more. They are decorative, characterful and charming. They did however create quite a mess at the

edges of the garden beds, tossing mulch as they went. I decided I didn't care. In fact, scratching the soil and all their droppings were wonderful for the garden. It was when we got our second dog, Lola, that we had to quickly reassess things, as she was a dreadful chicken chaser. No amount of training has deterred her. So we penned the chickens into the back of the garden near the compost bins. Lola spent hours staring at them through the fence, bingeing on what we called 'Chookflix'. I could hardly bear to look over the fence at them, as they looked so sad and put out. And they followed up with a boycott on egg production!

As the weather warmed, I decided that I was going to create a new garden area within

CHICKENS

their pen. I made a pond with rocks, irises and lilies. New garden beds emerged from this rather depressing part of the garden. I dug up the hardiest of plants from other parts of the garden (hellebores, oyster plants, euphorbia and salvias) to add to the new beds. I trimmed back the old leaning quince tree and tidied up the compost beds. Eventually I dragged in an old garden seat and, once again, got to sit happily in my new 'Chook Garden'. I'm not sure who was happier, me or the chickens. And to my joy… the very next day I got an egg!

Chickens will eat all your leftovers, garden weeds and lawn clippings. They eat slugs and bugs and mice and in return give you the best tasting eggs.

My advice to those who are thinking of getting chickens is to think how they are going to be housed. There are a million styles of chicken coops. Choose one that provides good laying boxes and has perches for resting at night. It absolutely must be foxproof. The chickens need to be kept away from the vegetable garden, as they will eat anything leafy.

There are lots of different breeds and, sorry to say, the dullest looking chickens are usually the worst layers. Most are good for three years or so and then they become rather seasonal in their egg laying and eventually they lay hardly any. At this point they just become your friends.

Bees

I only know a little about bees, but I do know that since we have had bees our garden has benefited enormously. Pollination is a vital part of a successful vegetable garden. Without bees not much will thrive. If you are interested in getting bees it is wise to check with your neighbours to see if they have allergies to bee stings. It is also important to do a course on beekeeping. It is very distressing if your hive becomes weak and then is invaded by another hive and robbed of all its honey, killing your bees as they go. Bees are extremely precious to us and they need proper care.

Some people choose to house a beehive in their garden and share the honey with a local beekeeper, who in return tends and checks the bees. I would highly recommend doing it this way. One of the ways you can play a part in your bees' welfare is by making sure there are plenty of very shallow water bowls for them to drink from. Anything too deep and they will drown. Rocks in bird baths are great. It is also worth knowing what flowers bees like. I find anything purple or yellow is a big winner.

Here are some of their favourites:

Borage
Zinnias
Coneflowers
Basil
Lavender
Black-eyed Susan
Poppies
Chive flowers
Marigolds
Blossom trees

Notes on the recipes

Sterilising jars

Sterilise jars and lids by washing them in soapy water and heating in the oven for 15 minutes at 160°C. Alternatively, boiling the jars and lids for 15 minutes will also suffice. The jam and the jars have to be of similar temperature when filling to prevent cracking.

Jam setting

When you're about to make jam, put a couple of saucers in the freezer for testing. When you think your jam might be ready, test it by dropping a teaspoon of jam on the very cold saucer. Return it to the freezer for 5 minutes, then push the jam with your finger. If it wrinkles, it's ready. If not, return the pan to the heat and boil for a further 5 minutes. Place the saucer back in the freezer ready to test the jam again. Keep cooking and testing every 5 minutes if neccessary. When set, turn off the heat and cool for 5 minutes. Using a sterilised funnel, pour the hot jam into the sterilised jars.

Olive oil

I often make reference to using a good quality extra virgin olive oil in my recipes and there is a very good reason for this. A good, rich and fruity oil can take a very simple dish to the next level. Almost all markets will have a good local olive oil producer. I think it is important to support these small producers and to taste all the different complexities that each olive oil offers. These growers are passionate about what they do and will talk you through the different flavour notes and how to pair them with certain foods. Sometimes these oils seem rather expensive but they can be used sparingly and still pack a punch in flavour. There are also some good extra virgin olive oils sold in supermarkets and delis that are less expensive and can be used liberally, especially when oil is needed for cooking rather than for drizzling. It's good to stock both types in your pantry.

Serving sizes

I am occasionally haphazard in my approach to recipes, including some featured in this book. Don't be too pedantic about some of the measurements in these recipes, especially where I suggest a handful or bunch of something. Taste things as you go and think about the pairing of flavours, how mellow or how intense you might want the dish to taste. These recipes are made to accommodate the fluctuations of harvest sizes and the amount of people you are going to feed. The recipes can be adjusted or altered to suit you. The only recipes that aren't suitable for change are cakes or the tart pastry.

Conversions

This book uses 20 ml (4 teaspoon) tablespoon measures. Please note that UK/US use 15 ml (3 teaspoon) tablespoon measures. The recipes also use conventional oven cooking temperatures. If you are using a fan-forced oven, please lower the temperature 20°C. Below is a table to help convert any measurements used throughout the book.

LENGTH

MM/CM	INCHES
3 mm	⅛ inch
4 mm	³⁄₁₆ inch
5–6 mm	¼ inch
1 cm	½ inch
2 cm	¾ inch
2.5 cm	1 inch
3 cm	1¼ inches
4 cm	1½ inches
5 cm	2 inches
6 cm	2½ inches
10 cm	4 inches
18 cm	7 inches
20 cm	8 inches
23 cm	9 inches
24 cm	9½ inches
25 cm	10 inches
30 cm	12 inches
40 cm	16 inches
50 cm	20 inches
1 m	40 inches

WEIGHT

G	OZ	LB
15 g	½ oz	
30 g	1 oz	
55 g	2 oz	
85 g	3 oz	
115 g	4 oz	¼ lb
140 g	5 oz	
175 g	6 oz	
200 g	7 oz	
225 g	8 oz	½ lb
250 g	9 oz	
310 g	11 oz	
350 g	12 oz	¾ lb
375 g	13 oz	
400 g	14 oz	
425 g	15 oz	
450 g	16 oz	1 lb
680 g	24 oz	1½ lb
900 g	32 oz	2 lb

LIQUID VOLUME

ML/LITRES	FL OZ	CUPS
30 ml	1 fl oz	⅛ cup
60 ml	2 fl oz	¼ cup
80 ml	2½ fl oz	⅓ cup
100 ml	3½ fl oz	
125 ml	4 fl oz	½ cup
160 ml	5 fl oz	⅔ cup
180 ml	6 fl oz	¾ cup
200 ml	7 fl oz	
250 ml	8 fl oz	1 cup
300 ml	10½ fl oz	
350 ml	12 fl oz	
400 ml	14 fl oz	
500 ml	16 fl oz	2 cups
1 litre	32 fl oz	4 cups

OVEN TEMPERATURES

°C	°F	GAS
70°C	150°F	¼
100°C	200°F	½
110°C	225°F	½
120°C	235°F	½
130°C	235°F	1
150°C	300°F	2
160°C	315°F	2–3
180°C	350°F	4
200°C	400°F	6
210°C	410°F	6–7
220°C	425°F	7
240°C	475°F	8

A note on climate zones

You might have noticed a zone name or number on some plant packets or in gardening books. This tells you which climate zone is best suited for the plant. Each plant has its own ideal conditions, some like a dry summer and others prefer the humidity. It's important to know your climate zone when planning and planting your kitchen garden, as it may affect what you're able to successfully grow. I recommend that you research plants that you're keen to grow and check if they are suitable for your area and when to plant them. A variety of plants can be grown all year round in some areas and seasonally in other areas.

You can find your climate zone online or in select books on the subject. They will be profiled with a number or by the name of your zone. The zone number is the standard by which gardeners can determine which plants are likely to thrive at a location. The hardiness zones are defined by the temperature range or humidity in that geographical area. Be cautious of microclimates, frosts and the variations that may come with each season. For example, if it is quite a cool summer then your tomatoes may not fruit as well as you expected, even though you checked your climate zone prior to planting.

The climate zones used in this book are cool, temperate and tropical. These are the three most common zones.

COOL: If you're living in a cool climate area, you are most likely experiencing very cold winters and heavy frosts. The summer period is short but can still be hot and dry.

TEMPERATE: This is the most common climate zone found across the world. Typically people living in the temperate zone will have cool winters, hot summers and experience all four seasons.

TROPICAL: These zones are usually hot, wet and have high humidity. They don't experience frosts and the winters are quite warm.

Most gardening fails are caused by gardeners not understanding the climate needs of their plants. Whether it be the right season, or the right aspect, climate is a big player in plant health. It's always a good idea to do a little prep work before you start growing your kitchen garden.

An easy way to start your planning your kitchen garden is to:

- Think about what plants you like to eat and cook with
- Check whether you are able to grow those plants in your climate zone
- Research those plants' companions and dislikes
- Find which herbs and flowers will help keep the pests away
- Consult your favourite planting chart (see my version on pp. 195–201) to determine which month is best to start growing your plants according to your climate

Note: The sowing and harvesting seasons for each fruit or vegetable entry indicate the most common seasons for each plant. For specific details on the best sowing season for your climate zone, please refer to the planting charts.

Chapter 07

Planting charts

Use these planting charts to help plan out your ideal kitchen garden. They include condensed information found throughout this book as well as the best seasons to plant according to your climate. For more information on climate zones see p. 192.

FRUIT / VEG	pH	SPACE	COMPANIONS	DISLIKES	WHEN TO PLANT		
					Cool	Temp	Trop
Apple	5.5–7.5	3 m	NA	NA	winter	winter	winter
Artichoke	6.8–7.5	1.5 m	broccoli, Brussels sprouts, cabbage, cauliflower, kohlrabi, turnips	none	spring	spring	spring
Asparagus	5.8–7.0	35 cm	carrots, basil, tomatoes, eggplant, dill	garlic, onions, potatoes	winter	winter	winter
Beans	6.8–7.5	20 cm	carrots, celery, cucumber, chard, eggplant, corn, peas, potatoes, pumpkin, parsley, celeriac, lettuce, spinach	beetroot, onions, chives	spring	spring	all year
Beetroot	5.8–7.0	10 cm	brassicas, kohlrabi, onions, silverbeet, cabbage	beans, tomatoes	spring, summer	winter, spring, summer	autumn, winter
Blackberries	6.8–7.5	1.5–3 m	peas, beans	tomatoes, potatoes, eggplant, capsicums, strawberries	winter, spring	winter, spring	not suitable
Blueberries	4.0–5.0	75 cm	basil, thyme, rhubarb	plants with pH above 6.0	winter, spring	winter, spring	not suitable
Bok choy	5.8–7.0	10 cm	beans, beetroot, onions, carrots, peas, potatoes	cauliflower, Brussels sprouts	spring, summer, autumn	winter, spring, summer	all year
Broad beans	5.8–7.0	30 cm	carrots, marigolds, eggplant, potatoes	beetroot, onions, garlic, sunflowers	autumn, spring	autumn, winter	autumn
Broccoli	5.8–7.0	35 cm	everything except dislikes	strawberries, tomatoes, capsicums, eggplant	spring, summer, autumn	summer, autumn	all year
Brussels Sprout	6.8–7.5	60 cm	everything except dislikes	tomatoes, strawberries, capsicums, eggplant	spring, summer, autumn	summer	not suitable

FRUIT / VEG	pH	SPACE	COMPANIONS	DISLIKES	WHEN TO PLANT		
					Cool	Temp	Trop
Cabbage	6.8–7.5	40 cm	everything except dislikes	tomatoes, strawberries, capsicums, eggplant	spring, summer, autumn	all year	all year
Cape Gooseberry	5.5–7.5	50 cm	basil, asparagus, carrots, chives, nasturtiums parsnips, borage, marigolds	rosemary, dill, potatoes, kohlrabi, fennel, strawberries	spring	spring	autumn, winter
Capsicum	6.8–7.5	40 cm	carrots, parsnips, tomatoes, eggplant, chillies	fennel, potatoes, bok choy, broccoli, Brussels sprouts, cauliflower, kale, kohlrabi, rocket, radishes	spring, summer	spring, summer	spring, summer, autumn
carrots	5.8–7.0	5 cm	beans, peas, capsicums, chillies, Brussels sprouts, kale, kohlrabi, chives, lettuce, leeks, sage, marigolds	dill, parsnips, celery, potatoes	spring, summer	all year	all year
Cauliflower	6.8–7.5	45 cm	everything except dislikes	tomatoes, strawberries, capsicums, eggplant	spring, summer	spring, summer, autumn	summer, autumn
celeriac	6.8–7.5	30 cm	beans, garlic, leeks, onions	carrots, corn, parsnips, potatoes, lettuce	spring	spring, summer, autumn	summer
Celery	6.8–7.5	30 cm	everything except dislikes	carrots, corn, parsnips, potatoes, lettuce	spring	spring, summer	summer
Cherries	6.0–6.5	3–4 m	NA	NA	winter	winter	winter
Chillies	6.8–7.5	40 cm	carrots, parsnips, tomatoes, eggplant, capsicums	fennel, potatoes	spring	spring	spring, summer, autumn
Citrus	5.5–7.5	3 m	NA	NA	autumn, winter, spring	autumn, winter, spring	all year

FRUIT / VEG	pH	SPACE	COMPANIONS	DISLIKES	WHEN TO PLANT		
					Cool	**Temp**	**Trop**
Corn	5.8–7.0	30 cm	beans, zucchini, cucumbers, pumpkins	tomatoes, celery, celeriac	spring	spring	winter, spring, summer
Crabapples	5.5–7.5	3 m	NA	NA	winter	winter	all year
Cucumber	6.8–7.5	30 cm	everything except dislikes	potatoes, tomatoes, sage	spring	spring	winter, spring, summer
Eggplant	4.5–5.8	60 cm	potatoes, peas, beans, capsicums, tomatoes	bok choy, brassicas	spring	spring	spring, summer
Fennel	6.8–7.5	30 cm	basil, dill	beans, broad beans, capsicums, tomatoes, coriander, eggplant	spring, summer	autumn, spring	autumn, winter
Figs	5.5–6.5	3 m	NA	NA	autumn, winter	autumn, winter	all year
Garlic	6.8–7.5	15–18 cm	everything except dislikes	beans, broad beans, peas	autumn, winter	autumn, winter	autumn, winter
Horse radish	5.5–7.5	50 cm	potatoes, sweet potatoes, strawberries, rhubarb	none	late spring	spring	winter
J. Artichoke	6.8–7.5	30 cm	everything except dislikes	beans, garlic, potatoes, tomatoes, onions, leeks, chives	spring	spring	spring
Kohlrabi	5.8–7.0	25 cm	beetroot, onions, marigolds, carrots, celery, silverbeet, cucumbers, garlic, lettuce, potatoes, basil, chives, artichokes, rhubarb, borage	tomatoes, strawberries, capsicums, eggplant	spring, summer	summer, autumn, winter	autumn
leeks	6.8–7.5	15 cm	everything except dislikes	beans, broad beans, peas, artichokes	spring, summer	spring, summer, autumn	autumn

FRUIT / VEG	pH	SPACE	COMPANIONS	DISLIKES	WHEN TO PLANT		
					Cool	Temp	Trop
Lettuce	5.8–7.0	15–25 cm	beetroot, carrots, parsnips, radishes, onions, broccoli	celery, cress, parsley	all year	all year	all year
Medlars	5.5–7.5	5 m	NA	NA	winter	winter	not suitable
Onions	6.8–7.5	10 cm	everything except dislikes	beans, broad beans, peas	autumn, winter	autumn, winter	autumn
Parsnips	6.8–7.5	20–30 cm	most things except dislikes	carrots, celery, celeriac	spring, summer	winter, spring, summer	autumn, winter
Passionfruit	6.8–7.5	1.5 m	nasturtiums, marigolds	none	spring, summer	spring, summer	all year
Pears	6.0–6.5	3–4 m	NA	NA	winter	winter	all year
Peas	5.8–7.0	20 cm	beans, cabbage, lettuce, carrots, beetroot	chives, garlic, onions	winter, spring	autumn, winter	autumn, winter
Plum	6.5	3–4 m	NA	NA	winter	winter	all year
Pomegranate	5.5–7.5	3 m	NA	NA	spring	spring	all year
Potatoes	6.8–7.5	45–70 cm	everything except dislikes	capsicums, carrots, celery, cucumbers, tomatoes, zucchini, apples, cherries, raspberries, strawberries, chillies, pumpkins, celeriac, spinach	spring	late winter, spring	summer, winter
Pumpkin	6.8–7.5	1 m	beans, corn, melons, zucchini	potatoes	spring	spring, early summer	spring, summer

FRUIT / VEG	pH	SPACE	COMPANIONS	DISLIKES	WHEN TO PLANT		
					Cool	Temp	Trop
Quince	5.5–7.5	3 m	NA	NA	winter	winter	all year
Radicchio	5.8–7.0	15–25 cm	beetroot, carrots, parsnips, radishes, onions	none	autumn	autumn	not suitable
Radish	5.5–7.5	5–10 cm	beetroot, carrots, celery, silverbeet, potatoes, peas	tomatoes, strawberries, capsicums, eggplant	all year	spring, summer, autumn	all year
Raspberries	6.8–7.5	30 cm	garlic, chives, nasturtiums, leeks	tomatoes, eggplant, potatoes	winter	winter	not suitable
Rhubarb	6.8–7.5	1 m	most things	none	spring	spring	not suitable
Spinach	5.8–7.0	15–20 cm	everything except dislikes	basil	autumn, winter, spring	autumn, winter, spring	autumn
Stone Fruit	6.0–7.0	3 m	NA	NA	winter	winter	all year
Strawberries	6.8–7.5	30 cm	lettuce, chives, sage, carrots	tomatoes, eggplant, potatoes, roses	spring	winter	autumn, winter
Turnip	5.8–7.0	20 cm	onions, peas, beetroot, Brussels sprouts, spinach, choy sum, garlic, leeks	potatoes, tomatoes, strawberries, eggplant	spring	summer	summer, autumn
tomatoes	5.5–7.5	90 cm	basil, asparagus, carrots, chives, nasturtiums, parsnips, borage, marigolds	rosemary, dill, potatoes, kohlrabi, fennel, strawberries	spring	spring, summer	all year
zucchini	5.5–7.5	1 m	beans, corn, peas, radishes	potatoes	spring	spring, summer	winter, spring, summer

HERB	pH	SPACE	COMPANIONS	DISLIKES	WHEN TO PLANT		
					Cool	Temp	Trop
Basil	5.5–7.5	25 cm	tomatoes	none	spring, summer	spring, summer	all year
Chamomile	5.5–7.5	20 cm	onions, broccoli	none	winter, spring	winter, spring	not suitable
Chervil	6.0–6.5	15 cm	everything	none	spring, summer	spring, summer	all year
Chives	6.0–7.0	5 cm	carrots	none	spring, summer, autumn	spring, summer, autumn	winter
Coriander	5.5–7.5	30 cm	dill, chervil, carrots	fennel	spring	spring	winter
Dill	5.5–7.5	15 cm	cabbage, tomatoes	none	spring	spring	winter
Lemon Balm	5.5–7.5	25 cm	everything	none	spring	spring	winter
Lemon Verbena	5.5–7.5	25 cm	everything	none	spring	spring	winter
Lovage	6–7.5	30 cm	potatoes	none	spring, summer	spring, summer	spring, summer
Mint	5.5–7.5	30 cm	tomatoes, cabbage	none	spring, summer	spring	winter
Oregano	5.5–7.5	15 cm	broccoli	none	spring, summer	spring, summer, autumn	winter

HERB	pH	SPACE	COMPANIONS	DISLIKES	WHEN TO PLANT		
					Cool	Temp	Trop
Parsley	5.5–7.5	20–30 cm	carrots, chives, tomatoes	potatoes	spring, summer, autumn	spring, summer, autumn	winter
Rosemary	6.0–7.5	50 cm	everything except dislikes	tomatoes, potatoes	spring	spring	spring
Sage	6.0–7.0	50 cm	everything	cucumber	spring	spring	spring
Sweet Marjoram	6.0–7.5	20 cm	capsicums	none	spring, summer	spring, summer	all year
Tarragon	6.5–7.0	40 cm	everything	none	spring	spring	spring
Thyme	6.5–7.0	30 cm	everything	none	spring	spring	spring

Index

Note: Bolded entries indicate plants that have individual profiles within the book.

Acknowledgements

I have many people I'd like to thank for this book but held up high and placed on a pedestal – even a garland around her neck – is my publisher, Kirsten Abbott. This book was her vision and her entrusting me to do this has been an absolute honour. I would also like to thank Lisa Schuurman, who gently held my hand throughout the editing stages. I'm very grateful for the energy that she brought to the whole process. It must have been quite an undertaking with my luddite skills. Her patience and cheerful demeanor kept the show on the road. I thank Jo Turner and Melody Lord as my editors. I am so thrilled with Ashlea O'Neill's contribution as my book designer. She brought a vibrant and easy to navigate format to the book. I couldn't have asked for a more respectful and inspired designer to work with. I would like to thank my husband, Julian, who took over all household and gardening chores enabling me to write and illustrate this book. It was a happy time as I worked away in my little garden studio for a solid eight months.

I was nicely supported by the loyal company of my two dogs, Digby and Lola, who fully embraced the life of an illustrator/author. Thank you also to my children, Lily and Fred, and their soon to be wedded partners, Jonny and Kirra, for their input and encouragement. All four have buckets of style and expertise, so are a trustworthy reference. And thank you to my dear mother, who always makes me feel like a superstar! I would like to thank the extremely clever cooks who gave me permission to use their recipes for this book: Gill Meller, Kathy Tsaples, Rodney Dunn, Séverine Demanet, Belinda Jeffery, Frank Fariello and Diana Georgeff.

I would also like to acknowledge Dja Dja Wurrung people past and present who are the traditional custodians of the land on which I wrote this book.

I've learnt it takes a village to get a book on the shelves… a village I'm full of gratitude for.

First published in Australia in 2022
by Thames & Hudson Australia Pty Ltd
11 Central Boulevard, Portside Business Park
Port Melbourne, Victoria 3207
ABN: 72 004 751 964

First published in the United Kingdom in 2022
by Thames & Hudson Ltd
181a High Holborn
London WC1V 7QX

First published in the United States of America in 2022
by Thames & Hudson Inc.
500 Fifth Avenue
New York, New York 10110

The Kitchen Garden © Thames & Hudson Australia 2022

Text and illustrations © Lucy Mora 2022

Recipes reprinted with permission:
p. 13 – Diana Georgeff's stuffed artichokes recipe
p. 30 – 'Imam Baldi' by Kathy Tsaples, *Sweet Greek:
    Simple Food & Sumptuous Feasts*, Melbourne Books,
    Australia, 2013
p. 33 – Frank Fariello's insalata di arance e
    finocchi recipe
p. 49 – The Agrarian Kitchen's sourdough potato cakes
p. 61 – 'Upside-down tomato and basil pie' by Belinda
    Jeffery, *Mix & Bake*, Lantern, Australia, 2017
p. 101 – Recipe adapted from Gill Meller's 'roast
    little gems with peas, peppercorns, parsley and
    cream', *Root, Stem, Leaf, Flower: How to cook with
    vegetables and other plants*, Quadrille, United
    Kingdom, 2020

25 24 23 22   5 4 3 2 1

The moral right of the author has been asserted.

Thames & Hudson Australia wishes to acknowledge that
Aboriginal and Torres Strait Islander people are the first
storytellers of this nation and the traditional custodians
of the land on which we live and work. We acknowledge
their continuing culture and pay respect to Elders past,
present and future.

ISBN 978-1-760-76232-2
ISBN 978-1-760-76290-2 (U.S. edition)

 A catalogue record for this
book is available from the
National Library of Australia

British Library Cataloguing-in-Publication Data
A catalogue record for this book is available from the
British Library

Library of Congress Control Number 2021952758

Every effort has been made to trace accurate ownership
of copyrighted text and visual materials used in this
book. Errors or omissions will be corrected in subsequent
editions, provided notification is sent to the publisher.

Design: Ashlea O'Neill | Salt Camp Studio
Series concept: Jo Turner
Editing: Melody Lord
Printed and bound in China by C&C Offset Printing
Co., Ltd

FSC® is dedicated to the promotion of responsible forest
management worldwide. This book is made of material
from FSC®-certified forests and other controlled sources.

Be the first to know about our new releases,
exclusive content and author events by visiting
thamesandhudson.com.au
thamesandhudson.com
thamesandhudsonusa.com